FAT QUARTER
Friendly

from Fons and Porter's
For the Love of Quilting Magazine

Fat Quarter Friendly

From Fons and Porter's For the Love of Quilting

©2000 by Oxmoor House, Inc.
Book Division of Southern Progress Corporation
P.O. Box 2463, Birmingham, Alabama 35201

Published by Oxmoor House, Inc., and Leisure Arts, Inc.

Library of Congress Catalog Card Number: 99-085954
Hardcover ISBN: 0-8487-2369-4
Softcover ISBN: 0-8487-2361-9
Manufactured in the United States of America
Second Printing 2000

Editor-in-Chief: Nancy Fitzpatrick Wyatt
Senior Crafts Editor: Susan Ramey Cleveland
Senior Editor, Copy and Homes: Olivia Kindig Wells
Art Director: James Boone

Fat Quarter Friendly

From *Fons and Porter's For the Love of Quilting*

Editor: Rhonda Richards
Contributing Technical Writer: Laura Morris Edwards
Contributing Pattern Tester: Patricia Everman Myers
Copy Editor: Amanda Owens
Editorial Assistant: Suzanne Powell
Contributing Designer: Carol Damsky
Illustrator: Kelly Davis
Senior Photographer: John O'Hagan
Contributing Photographer: Keith Harrelson
Photo Stylist: Linda Baltzell Wright
Director, Production and Distribution: Phillip Lee
Associate Production Manager: Kaye Smith
Production Assistant: Faye Porter Bonner

We would like to express thanks to Terry Cates and Cindy Wilson, owners of Heart to Heart Quilt Shop in Trussville, Alabama, for use of their shop to shoot the cover and fat quarters shown throughout this book.
Heart to Heart Quilt Shop
1110 North Chalkville Road
Trussville, Alabama 35173
(205) 661-0537

From Liz and Marianne

We buy fat quarters, pieces of fabric about 18" x 22", almost every place we shop. We pick up these useful pieces of fabric in bundles of color-coordinated prints; of a new designer's line; of Halloween, Christmas, or other holiday fabrics; and of plaids, flannels, batiks, and other themed groupings. Often these bundles, sporting ribbon or raffia bows, are so appealing that we just can't resist them.

With the popularity of scrap quilts, the emphasis in our fabric stashes is now on the variety of fabrics we have, rather than on the quantity of any individual fabric. But now that we have all those wonderful fat quarters, what are we going to do with them?

Well, we have come up with an answer. In our magazine, *Fons and Porter's For the Love of Quilting,* we label many of our projects as "Fat Quarter Friendly," meaning that these quilts are uniquely suited to using fat quarters of fabric. You don't have to worry if fat quarters are large enough to cut the shapes you need and give you the needed number of pieces. In some cases, we also label projects as "Fat Eighth Friendly," meaning 9" x 22" fabric pieces will work for this project.

This book features a collection of our most popular Fat Quarter Friendly and Fat Eighth Friendly quilts from the magazine. Now, when you have the urge to pull a bundle of fat quarters off your shelf, you have 30 patterns at your fingertips to inspire you.

We hope that you enjoy this collection and that you will start using those wonderful fat quarters to make quilts!

◈ Contents ◈

In the Sewing Room

5

Dresden on the Half Shell

A friend gave Bette Lee Collins a stack of 1930s Dresden Plate blocks. Bette appliquéd the yellow centers and created the scrappy setting and border with authentic 1930s fabrics. "The half-shell (or clamshell) quilting seemed to give the quilt a continuous motion that I liked," says Bette. She combined the block name and quilting pattern name to dub her quilt, "Dresden on the Half Shell."

Finished Size: 70" x 87"
Blocks: 12 (15") Dresden
Plate Blocks

Materials

24 fat quarters* assorted
    1930s prints for blocks and
    borders
1/8 yard medium green plaid
    for stems
1/4 yard yellow for sashing
    squares and appliqué
4 3/4 yards white for back-
    ground
5 1/2 yards fabric for backing
5/8 yard small green plaid for
    binding
Template plastic
Full-size batting
* Fat quarter = 18" x 22"

Cutting

Measurements include 1/4"
seam allowances. Cut crosswise strips unless otherwise
noted. Make templates for patterns A and B, leaf, small circle, small posy, medium posy,
and large posy on page 9.

From assorted 1930s
prints, cut:
• 192 As.

• 220 (2 1/2" x 4 1/4") rectangles
  for sashing and pieced
  borders.
• 128 leaves.
• 4 large posies.
• 22 medium posies.
• 18 small posies.

From medium green
plaid, cut:
• 4 (7/8"-wide) strips. Fold strips
  in thirds so they are approximately 1/4"-wide and press.
  Cut strips into 14 (9"-long)
  stem pieces.

From yellow, cut:
• 12 Bs.
• 22 small circles for posy
  centers.
• 6 (2 1/2") squares for sashing
  squares.

From white, cut:
• 2 yards. Cut 2 (7" x 70 1/2")
  lengthwise strips for side
  borders and 2 (7" x 66 1/2")
  lengthwise strips for top and
  bottom borders.
• From remainder, cut 12
  (15 1/2") background squares.

From small green plaid, cut:
• 9 (2 1/4"-wide) strips for
  binding.

Block Assembly

1. Join 16 As to form a circle. Baste under 1/4" seam allowance around outer edge. **2.** Fold and crease background squares to make appliqué guidelines. Center and pin A circle on background square. Baste under 1/4" around B. Center B over center of A circle. Appliqué A and B to background. Make 12 blocks (*Dresden Block Diagram*). Turn block over and carefully trim background fabric from behind A and B, leaving 1/4" seam allowance.

→

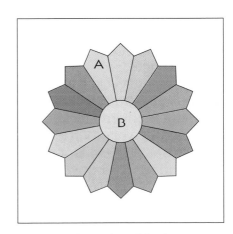

**Dresden Block
Diagram**

Cumberland Mountain

"When our Cumberland fabrics for Benartex were printed, it felt like Christmas in August," says Liz Porter. "Pieces arrived almost daily straight from the mill. I began using the fabric immediately to make this quilt. Day one brought the tan leaf print I used as the background. I added the medium and dark fabrics as they arrived. By cutting and piecing a few blocks each day, I had my top done by the end of the month."

Finished Size: 72" x 84"
Blocks: 120 (6") Blocks

Materials
40 fat eighths* assorted
    medium and dark prints
    for blocks
2¼ yards light print for blocks
2¼ yards green print for
    borders and binding
5 yards fabric for backing
Full-size batting
*Fat eighth = 9" x 22"

Cutting
Measurements include ¼"
seam allowances. Border
strips are exact length needed.
You may want to cut them
longer to allow for piecing
variations.

*I used about 40 fat eighths
(9" x 22"). I cut at least 1 (6⅞")
square from each and up to 3
from others for B. Then I cut
180 (2⅞") squares from the
remainder. —Liz*

From assorted medium and
dark prints, cut:
• 180 (2⅞") squares. Cut
  squares in half diagonally to
  make 360 half-square triangles (A).
• 60 (6⅞") squares. Cut
  squares in half diagonally to
  make 120 half-square
  triangles (B).

From light print, cut:
• 26 (2⅞"-wide) strips. Cut
  strips into 360 (2⅞") squares.
  Cut squares in half diagonally to make 720 half-square
  triangles (A).

**Triangle-Square
Diagram**

Piecing Diagram

From green print, cut:
• 8 (6½"-wide) strips. Piece
  strips to make 4 (6½" x
  72½") borders.
• 9 (2¼"-wide) strips for
  binding.

Block Assembly
1. Join 1 light A to 1 dark A.
Make 3 A triangle-squares
(*Triangle-Square Diagram*).
2. Arrange 3 light A triangles
and 3 A triangle-squares as
shown in *Piecing Diagram*.
Join as shown to make 1 triangle unit.
3. Join triangle unit with 1 B
triangle as shown in *Block
Assembly Diagram* to com-
plete block. ➞

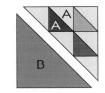

**Block Assembly
Diagram**

*B*efore joining the B triangle to the A triangle unit, fold both in half and pinch to find the center of the long side. Align the center points before stitching. —Marianne

4. Make 120 blocks (*Block Diagram*).

Quilt Assembly

1. Join 4 blocks into 1 block unit as shown in *Block Unit Diagram*. Make 30 block units.
2. Arrange block units into 6 horizontal rows of 5 units each as shown in *Row Assembly Diagram*. Join into rows; join rows to complete center.
3. Add green side borders; then add green top and bottom borders (*Quilt Top Assembly Diagram*).

Quilting and Finishing

1. Divide backing fabric into 2 (2½-yard) lengths. Cut 1 piece in half lengthwise. Sew 1 narrow panel to each side of wide panel. Press seam allowance toward narrow panels.
2. Layer backing, batting, and quilt top; baste. Quilt as desired. Quilt shown was machine-quilted with waves through small triangles and a looping pattern through large triangles. Side triangles have a leaf pattern and outer border has a leaf garland pattern.
3. Join 2¼"-wide green strips into 1 continuous piece for straight-grain French-fold binding. Add binding to quilt.

Block Diagram

Block Unit Diagram

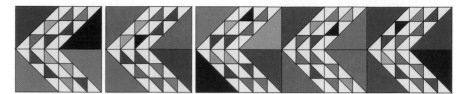

Row Assembly Diagram

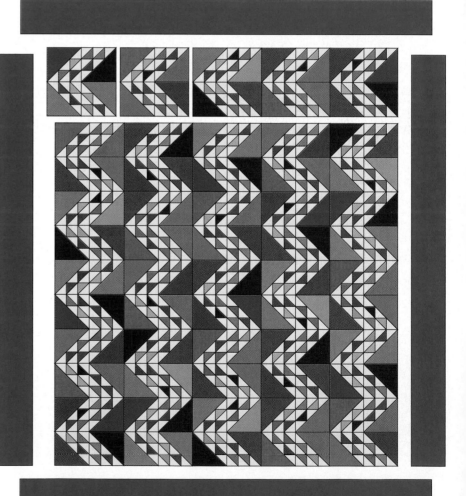

Quilt Top Assembly Diagram

Quilt by Liz Porter; quilted by New Traditions

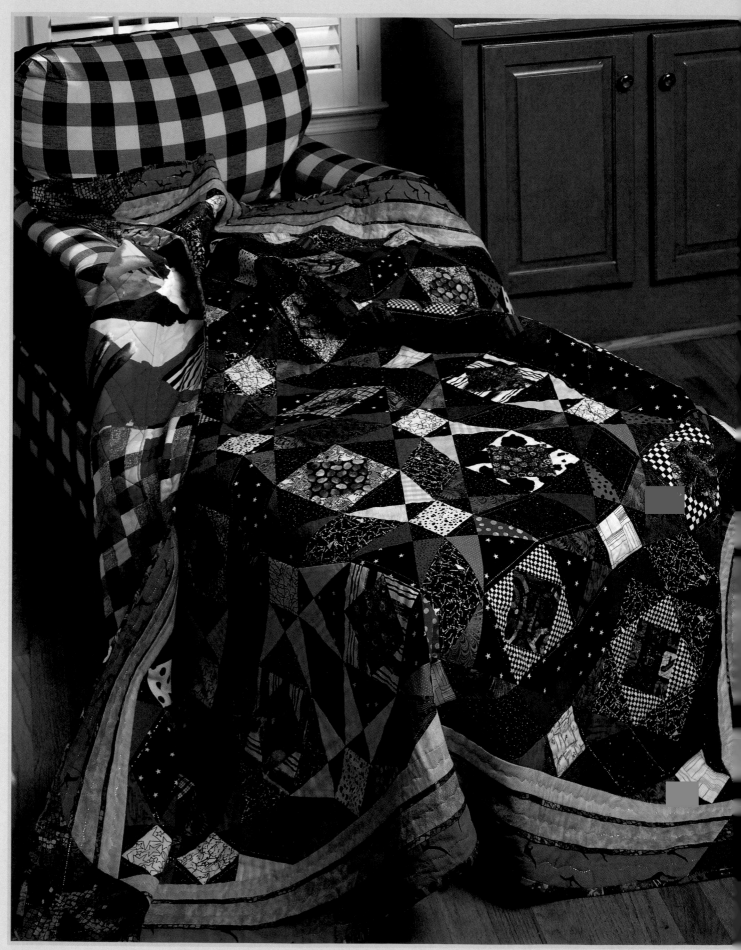

Rainbow After the Storm

For her Storm at Sea variation, Delaware quilter Vicki Schwam departed widely from the traditional blue and white color scheme.

Finished Size: 70" x 70"
Blocks: 36 (3¾")
Small Blocks,
25 (7½") Large Blocks,
60 (3¾" x 7½") Rectangles

Materials

6 fat eighths* (¾ yard total) white prints (A)
7 fat eighths* (⅞ yard total) medium-value white-with-black prints (D)
¾ yard each (4½ yards total) of 6 assorted black prints (B, E, F)
5 fat eighths* each assorted yellow, orange, red, pink, purple, blue, green prints (G)
12 fat eighths* or 25 scraps at least 4½"-square assorted primary colors-on-black prints (C)
½ yard each light and light/medium gray prints for borders
⅝ yard medium gray print for borders
1 yard dark gray print for border corners and piping
½ yard primary-on-gray print for binding
4½ yards fabric for backing
Twin-size batting
Freezer paper
*Fat eighth = 9" x 22"

Template Cutting

1. From freezer paper, cut 60 (3¾" x 7½") rectangles.
2. Fold each freezer-paper rectangle slightly to find center of sides.
3. Using rotary cutter and ruler, cut each rectangle into 5 freezer-paper templates as shown in *Freezer Paper Diagram*: 1 F diamond, 2 G triangles, and 2 G rev.

Freezer Paper Diagram

4. To use templates in instructions below, press templates to wrong side of fabrics, allowing ½" between each template. Cut out fabric pieces with rotary cutter and ruler, adding ¼" seam allowance beyond paper edge as you cut (see photo below). Do not remove paper.

Fabric Cutting

Measurements include ¼" seam allowances. Cut crosswise strips unless otherwise noted.

From assorted white prints, cut:
• 36 (4¼") squares total (A).

From assorted medium-value white-with-black prints, cut:
• 25 sets of 2 matching 3½" squares. Cut each square in half diagonally to make 25 sets of 4 matching triangles (D) for a total of 100 Ds.

From assorted black-with-white prints, cut:
• 36 sets of 4 matching 2⅜" squares (B). You will have 144 total.
• 25 sets of 2 matching 4⅝" squares. Cut each square in half diagonally to make 25 sets of 4 matching triangles (E). You will have 100 total.
• 60 F diamonds using freezer-paper templates.

From assorted yellow, orange, red, and pink prints, cut from each:
• 16 G triangles and 16 G rev. using freezer-paper templates.

From assorted purple and green prints, cut from each:
• 18 G triangles and 18 G rev. using freezer-paper templates.

➔

From assorted blue prints, cut:
- 20 G triangles and 20 G rev. using freezer-paper templates.

From assorted primary color-on-black prints, cut:
- 25 (4¼") squares (C).

From light gray, cut:
- 7 (1¾"-wide) strips. Cut 1 strip in half. Piece to make 2 (1¾" x 60½") strips and 2 (1¾" x 70½") strips for first border.

From light/medium gray, cut:
- 7 (2¼"-wide) strips. Cut 1 strip in half. Piece to make 2 (2¼" x 60½") strips and 2 (2½" x 70½") strips for second border.

From medium gray, cut:
- 7 (2½"-wide) strips. Cut 1 strip in half. Piece to make 2 (2½" x 60½") strips and 2 (2½" x 70½") strips for third border.

From dark gray, cut:
- 1 (10½"-wide) strip. Cut strip into 4 (10½") squares for border corners.
- 14 (1⅛"-wide) strips. Piece to make 4 (1⅛" x 60½") strips and 4 (1⅛" x 70½") strips. Fold in half lengthwise, wrong sides facing, and press to make unfilled piping borders.

From primary-on-gray, cut:
- 8 (2¼"-wide) strips for binding.

Block Assembly

1. Choose 1 A square and 1 set of 4 B squares. Referring to *Diagonal Seams Diagrams*, join 2 B squares to opposite sides of A square. Trim

— Small Block Diagram

Diagonal Seams Diagrams

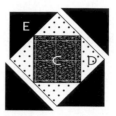

Large Block Piecing Diagram

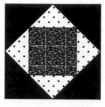

Large Block Diagram

Quilt Top Assembly Diagram

excess. Open out triangles. Press. Repeat by joining 2 B squares to remaining sides of A to complete unit (*Small Block Diagram*). Make 36 small blocks.

2. Choose 1 C square, 1 set of 4 D triangles, and 1 set of 4 E triangles. Referring to *Large Block Piecing Diagram*, join 2 D triangles to opposite sides of C square. Join 2 D triangles to remaining sides of C. Repeat with E triangles to complete block (*Large Block Diagram*). Make 25 large blocks.

It helps to fold the E triangles in half and pinch to find the center of the long side. Match the center to the corner of C. Stitch from the C side, sewing through the X made by the previous stitching. —Marianne

Diamond Rectangle Assembly

Carefully placed colors form diagonal rainbow bands across this quilt. You must refer closely to the *Quilt Top Assembly Diagram* as you construct and lay out pieced diamond rectangle units to form diagonal bands.

1. For the top left diamond rectangle unit in Row 1, select 1 F diamond, 2 red print G triangles, and 2 blue print G rev. triangles.

Don't let the G and G rev. templates confuse you! Because you press the freezer-paper templates to the wrong side of the fabric, the shapes reverse during the cutting process. —Marianne

2. Join red print G triangles to 2 opposite sides of F diamond. Pinmatch points of freezer paper templates to align pieces properly. Sew along edge of freezer paper. Open out and finger-press seams. Repeat to add blue print G rev. to remaining 2 opposite sides of diamond. Remove freezer paper and press.
3. Referring to *Quilt Top Assembly Diagram* for color placement, add G and G rev. triangles to F diamonds to form 60 units needed for quilt. Note that most units use 2 col-

ors per unit. Five units call for all 4 triangles to be the same color.

Quilt Assembly

1. Referring to *Quilt Top Assembly Diagram*, lay out small blocks, large blocks, and diamond rectangle units as shown. Carefully position rectangles to form rainbow stripes. Join blocks into rows; join rows to complete quilt center.
2. Pin 1 (60½") unfilled piping border in place along 1 edge of 1 (60½") light gray first border strip. Baste. Layer 2¼" x 60½" second light/medium gray border, right sides facing, and stitch along length. Press piping to inner border. Pin and baste second piping border to second border along 60½" edge. Layer third 60½" medium gray border and stitch along length. Press piping to second border. Repeat to make 2 (60½") border sections

and 2 (70½") border sections.
3. Join 2 shorter border sections to 2 opposite sides of quilt top. Join longer border sections to remaining 2 sides.
4. Place 1 border corner square on 1 corner of quilt. Stitch diagonally from 1 corner of square to opposite corner. Trim excess and open to reveal triangle. Repeat for remaining 3 corners.

Quilting and Finishing

1. Divide backing into 2 (2¼-yard) pieces. Cut 1 piece in half lengthwise. Join narrow panels to sides of wide panel to complete backing.
2. Layer backing, batting, and quilt top; baste. Quilt as desired. Quilt shown was machine-quilted with metallic thread.
3. Join 2¼"-wide binding strips into 1 continuous piece to make straight-grain French-fold binding. Add binding to quilt.

Quilt by Vicki Schwam

Double T

T-Blocks were a popular symbol of the Temperance Movement, an effort by many women of the 19th century to abolish alcohol. Diane Burdin was attracted to the pattern after seeing an antique quilt displayed at a local book store. In keeping with quilts of this period, Diane varied the placement of lights and darks in her patchwork, making "maverick" blocks that keep the pattern interesting.

Finished Size: 66" x 81¾"
Blocks: 20 (12¾") T-Blocks

Materials
15 fat eighths* assorted solids for blocks
20 fat eighths* assorted prints for blocks
⅜ yard solid chrome orange for sashing squares
1¾ yards brown print for sashing strips
¾ yard dark brown print for binding
5 yards fabric for backing
Twin-size batting
*Fat eighth = 9" x 22"

Cutting
Measurements include ¼" seam allowances. Cut crosswise strips unless otherwise noted. In this scrap quilt, you will see that there are several blocks that have 1 odd piece or 1 odd T in them. Instructions are given for matching blocks, but have fun and mix them if you like.

From assorted solids, cut:
• 80 (2" x 5") rectangles (A) in sets of 4.
• 160 (2½") squares (B) in sets of 8.

From each assorted print, cut:
• 8 (2" x 5") rectangles (A).
• 1 (5") square (C).
• 1 (7⅝") square. Cut squares in quarters diagonally to make 4 quarter-square triangles (D).
• 2 (4⅛") squares. Cut squares in half diagonally to make 4 half-square triangles (E).

From chrome orange, cut:
• 3 (3½"-wide) strips. Cut strips into 30 (3½") squares for sashing squares.

From brown print, cut:
• 17 (3½"-wide) strips. Cut strips into 49 (3½" x 13¼") rectangles for sashing strips.

From dark brown print, cut:
• 8 (2¼"-wide) strips for binding.

Block Assembly
1. Choose 2 print As and 1 solid A. Join along long sides to make a square as shown in *Unit A Diagram*. Make 4 A units.
2. Using diagonal-seams method and referring to *Unit B Diagram*, place 1 solid B atop corner of A unit as shown.

Stitch diagonally and trim excess. Press back to reveal triangle. Repeat at other corner to complete T unit, as shown in *T Unit Diagram*. Make 4 T units.
3. Referring to *Block Assembly Diagram*, lay out 4 T units, 1 C, 4 Ds, and 4 Es. Join in diagonal rows; join rows to complete block (*Block Diagram*).
4. Make 20 T-blocks. ➡

Unit A Diagram

Unit B Diagram

T Unit Diagram

Block Assembly Diagram

Block Diagram

◈ Double T

Quilt Assembly

1. Referring to *Block Row Diagram*, alternate 4 blocks with 5 sashing rectangles. Join into a block row. Make 5 block rows.

2. Referring to *Sashing Row Diagram*, join 5 sashing squares and 4 sashing strips into a sashing row. Make 6 sashing rows.

3. Alternate sashing rows and block rows. Join rows, matching seams, to complete quilt top.

Quilting and Finishing

1. Divide backing fabric into 2 (2½-yard) lengths. Divide 1 panel in half lengthwise. Sew 1 narrow panel to each side of wide panel to complete backing.

2. Layer backing, batting, and quilt top; baste. Quilt as desired. Quilt shown was quilted in-the-ditch. Sashing has a French cross/fleur-de-lis alternating pattern.

3. Join 2¼"-wide brown print strips into 1 continuous piece for straight-grain French-fold binding. Add binding to quilt.

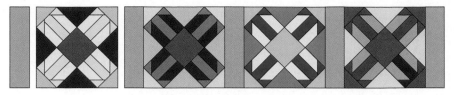

Block Row Diagram

Sashing Row Diagram

Quilt by Diane Burdin

Working with Bias Edges
by Rhonda Richards

I made a version of Diane Burdin's Double T quilt in a much different color scheme as a birthday gift for my sister, Teresa R. Jacobs. In the process of making blocks, I discovered a tip that might help you, too.

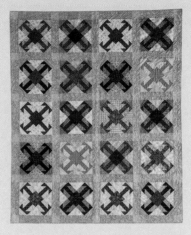

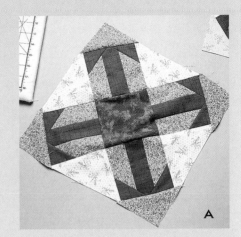

As I was making blocks, I found that most came out just perfectly. A few, however, were a little wobbly in the center (*photo* **A**). Rather than lying flat, the center area raised off the table a bit. I discovered that I was not handling the D pieces carefully. Those triangles have bias edges on two sides. As I was sewing and then pressing, I was stretching them out of shape just enough that my block would not lie flat. But I'm not one to start over or waste fabric!

To fix this problem, I pinned each corner of the block to a ruled ironing surface (*photo* **B**). This ensures that you don't stretch your block beyond the size it's supposed to be. Then I sprayed enough starch on the block to make it damp (*photo* **C**). If you don't like to use starch, mist your block with water. Then I used the iron set on "steam" to gently press the block flat and to size (*photo* **D**). Begin in the center, and slowly move outward to press it flat. The steam will reshape your block and redistribute the "roomy" areas.

When I was done, all my blocks lay flat (*photo* **E**). Use this trick with care; if you get carried away, you'll stretch your entire block out of shape and make it too large. But with a little careful pressing, you can repair minor mistakes.

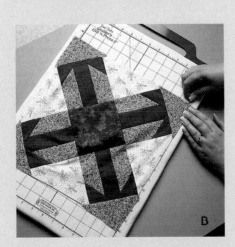

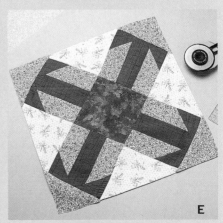

Oak Leaf

Marianne Fons (below left) and Liz Porter (below right) bought a bundle of fat quarters of beautiful brushed homespun fabrics at Quilt Market one fall. "Sometimes we buy fabrics on impulse just because we like them, not because we know how we'll use them," says Marianne. "One snowy winter day at Liz's house, we dropped everything to start the Oak Leaf quilt we had long wanted to make."

Finished Size:
82" x 100" Blocks:
20 (16") Oak Leaf
Blocks

Materials
Note: All fabrics in quilt shown are brushed homespun.

20 fat quarters* assorted light and medium prints for

appliqué block backgrounds
12-15 fat quarters* assorted light and medium prints for border
30 fat quarters* assorted dark prints for appliqué, pieced

border, and pieced sashing
¾ yard green for binding
7½ yards fabric for backing
Paper-backed fusible web
Queen-size batting
*Fat quarter = 18" x 22"

*W*e prewashed and dried
our brushed homespuns.
Then we stabilized the fabrics
before cutting by spraying
starch on the less-fuzzy side.

Cutting
Measurements include ¼"
seam allowances. Cut crosswise strips unless otherwise
noted. Liz and Marianne fused
appliqué shapes to back-
ground squares before button-
hole-stitching around pieces
(see page 25).

From assorted light and medium prints, cut:
• 20 (16½") squares for
  appliqué block backgrounds.
• 4 (6½") squares for border
  corners.
• 18 (2½" x 22") strips for middle border.
• 288 (2⅞") squares. Cut
  squares in half diagonally to
  make 576 half-square triangles for borders and sashing.

From assorted dark prints, cut:
• 20 sets (color combinations
  your choice) of:
  • 1 center (A).
  • 4 matching arcs (B).
  • 4 matching oak leaves (C).
  • 4 matching small leaves (D).
• 4 different oak leaves (C) for
  border corners.
• 288 (2⅞") squares. Cut
  squares in half diagonally to
  make 576 half-square triangles for borders and sashing.

From green stripe, cut:
• 9 (2¼"-wide) strips for
  binding.

Block Assembly
1. Follow instructions for
"*Window Fusible Appliqué*" on
page 25 to prepare shapes for
fusing. Referring to *Block
Diagram*, arrange 1 A, 4 matching Bs, 4 matching Cs, and 4
matching Ds on 1 (16½")
square. Fuse in alphabetical

Block Diagram

order, and then hand- or
machine-buttonhole-stitch in
place.
2. Make 20 Oak Leaf blocks.
3. Machine-buttonhole-stitch 1
oak leaf (C) on each 6½"
square (border corners).

Border Assembly
1. Join 1 light half-square
triangle with 1 dark half-square
triangle to make a triangle
square border unit. Repeat to
make 576 border units.
2. Checking directions of triangles against *Quilt Top
Assembly Diagram*, join 8 units
into a vertical sashing strip.
Make 15 strips.
3. Make 8 strips of 35 units
each (top and bottom borders,
horizontal sashing strips).
4. Make 4 strips of 44 units
each (side borders). ➞

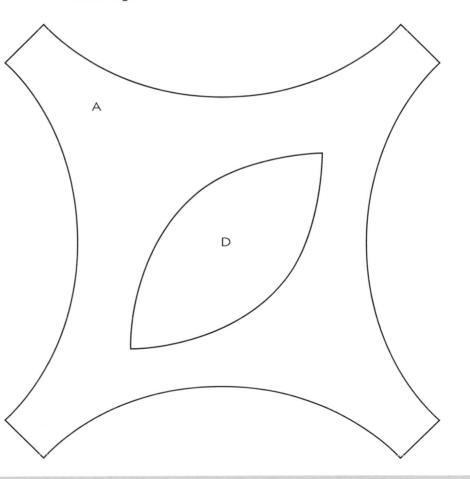

Plaid Pinwheels

"Pinwheels are among my favorite block patterns," says Lauren Caswell Brooks. "To really make the pinwheels show up against all these busy plaids, I kept my pinwheel triangles the same fabric in the center of each block and went scrappy on the outer pieces."

Finished Size: 40" x 50"
Blocks: 20 (10") Pinwheel
Blocks

Materials

16 to 20 fat eighths* (1 ½ yards total) assorted light to medium plaids and stripes for blocks
16 to 20 fat eighths* (1 ½ yard total) assorted medium to dark plaids and stripes for blocks
½ yard solid blue for binding
1 ½ yards fabric for backing
Crib-size batting
*Fat eighth = 9" x 22"

Cutting

Mix dark and light B pieces as desired. Measurements include ¼" seam allowances.

From light to medium plaids and stripes, cut:
• 20 sets of 2 (2⅞") squares. Cut squares in half diagonally to make 20 sets of 4 half-square triangles (A).
• 80 assorted B rev.

From medium to dark plaids and stripes, cut:
• 20 sets of 2 (2⅞") squares. Cut squares in half diagonally to make 20 sets of 4 half-square triangles (A).
• 80 assorted Bs.

From blue, cut:
• 5 (2¼"-wide) strips for binding.

Block Assembly

1. Choose 1 set each of light and dark A triangles. Choose 4 assorted dark Bs and 4 assorted light B rev.
2. Join 1 light A to 1 dark B. Join 1 dark A to 1 light B rev. Join units to make 1 quarter-block unit as shown in *Piecing Diagram*.
3. Make 4 quarter-block units as shown in *Block Assembly Diagram*. Join as shown in *Block Diagram* to complete 1 Pinwheel block.
4. Make 20 Pinwheel blocks. ➤

Piecing Diagram

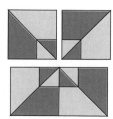

Block Assembly Diagram

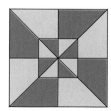

Block Diagram

Quilt Assembly

1. Referring to *Row Assembly Diagram* and photo, lay out blocks in 5 horizontal rows of 4 blocks each.

2. Join into rows; join rows to complete quilt.

Quilting and Finishing

1. Layer backing, batting, and quilt top; baste. Quilt as desired. Quilt shown was machine-quilted in an all-over leaf pattern.

2. Join 2¼"-wide solid blue strips into 1 continuous piece for straight-grain French-fold binding. Add binding to quilt.

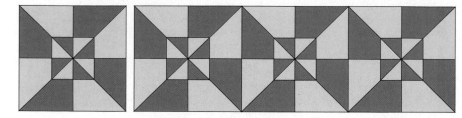

Row Assembly Diagram

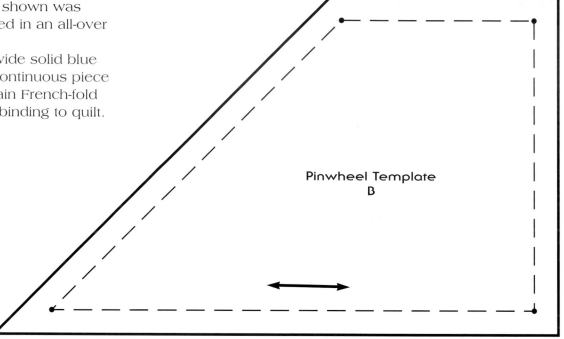

Pinwheel Template
B

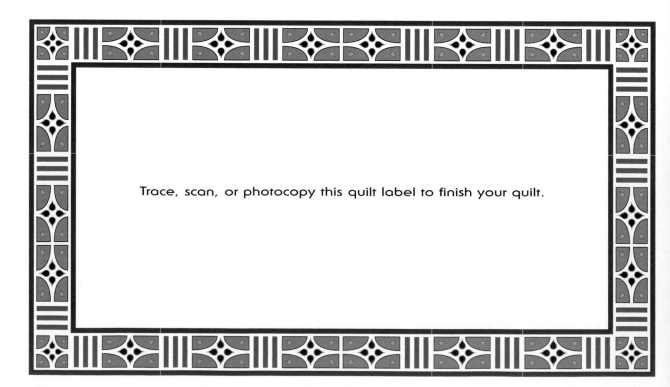

Trace, scan, or photocopy this quilt label to finish your quilt.

Quilt by Lauren Caswell Brooks; quilted by New Traditions

Memories

Several years ago, Linda Winter purchased boxes of feedsacks at the sale of her great aunt's estate. Linda wanted to create a quilt in memory of her aunt, Alma Esslinger, with those fabrics using a period pattern. Leafing through some old copies of the *Kansas City Star*, she found a pattern called "Our Country" that she adapted to make this quilt. "I quilted a wild rose trellis in the borders," says Linda, "because my aunt always had beautiful rose gardens."

Finished Size:
100½" x 100½"
Blocks: 20 (14") Cross Blocks and 16 (14") Setting Blocks

Materials
28 fat eighths* of assorted light 1930s prints for blocks
20 fat eighths* of assorted medium/dark 1930s prints for blocks
7 yards white for background
½ yard blue 1930s print for inner border
1¾ yards pink 1930s print for outer border and binding
9 yards fabric for backing
King-size batting
Template plastic
*Fat eighth = 9" x 22"

Cutting
Measurements include ¼" seam allowances. Cut crosswise strips unless otherwise noted. Make templates for patterns B and C on page 33.

From each light 1930s fat eighth, cut:
• 7 (2½") squares (A), for a total of 196 As.
• 7 (2⅞") squares. Cut squares in half diagonally to make a total of 392 half-square triangles (D).

From each medium/dark 1930s fat eighth, cut:
• 9 (2½") squares (A).
• 4 Bs.
• 4 (2⅞") squares. Cut squares in half diagonally to make 8 half-square triangles (D). (You will have 20 sets.)

From white, cut:
• 26 (2½"-wide) strips. Cut strips into 436 (2½") squares (A).
• 80 Cs.
• 80 C rev.
• 20 (2⅞"-wide) strips. Cut strips into 276 (2⅞") squares. Cut squares in half diagonally to make 552 half-square triangles (D).
• 10 (4½"-wide) strips. Cut strips into 56 (4½" x 6½") rectangles (E).
• 3 (14½"-wide) strips. Cut strips into 16 (6½" x 14½") rectangles (F).

From blue 1930s print, cut:
• 10 (1½"-wide) strips. Cut 2 strips in half. Join 2 strips plus 1 half strip to make border. Repeat to make 4 borders.

From pink 1930s print, cut:
• 10 (3¾"-wide) strips. Cut 2 strips in half. Join 2 strips plus 1 half strip to make border. Repeat to make 4 borders.
• 11 (2¼"-wide) strips for binding.

Cross Block Assembly
1. Join 5 matching medium print A squares and 4 white A squares into a block as shown (*Center Nine-Patch Unit Diagram*).
2. Join 1 matching medium print B, 1 white C, and 1 white C rev. as shown (*Point Unit Diagram*). Join 1 matching ➡

Center Nine-Patch Unit Diagram

Point Unit Diagram

medium print D and 1 white D into a half-square triangle unit. Make 2 half-square triangle units. Join Point Unit, half-square triangle units, 1 matching medium print A, and 2 white As as shown (*Side Unit Diagram*). Make 4 matching Side Units.

3. Using assorted light 1930s prints, join 1 print D to 1 white D to make a half-square triangle unit. Make 2 units. Join with 1 print A and 1 white A as shown (*Corner Unit Diagram*). Make 4 Corner Units.

4. Referring to *Cross Block Assembly Diagram*, join 1 Center Nine-Patch Unit, 4 Side Units, and 4 Corner Units to make 1 block. Make 20 Cross blocks.

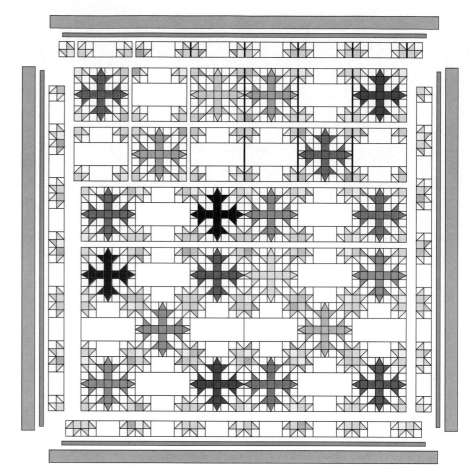

Quilt Top Assembly Diagram

Side Unit Diagram

Corner Unit Diagram

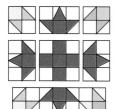

Cross Block Assembly Diagram

Cross Block Diagram

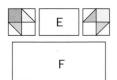

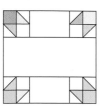

Setting Block Assembly Diagram

Setting Block Diagram

Setting Block Assembly

1. Make 4 Corner Units as above in assorted light 1930s prints. Join with 2 white Es and 1 white F as shown in *Setting Block Assembly Diagram* to make 1 Setting Block.

2. Make 16 Setting Blocks (*Setting Block Diagram*).

Border Unit Assembly

1. Make 52 Corner Units as above in assorted light 1930s prints. Join 1 Corner Unit to

Border Unit Assembly Diagram

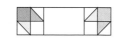

Border Unit Diagram

each end of 1 white E rectangle as shown (*Border Unit Assembly Diagram*). Make 24 Border Units.

2. The 4 remaining Corner Units will be border corners.

Quilt Assembly

1. Lay out blocks as shown in *Quilt Top Assembly Diagram* in 6 horizontal rows of 6 blocks each. Join into rows; join rows to complete center.

2. Join Border Units into 4 strips of 6 units as shown. Add 1 strip to each side of quilt, matching seams. Add remaining Corner Units to each end of remaining border strips. Add to top and bottom of quilt, matching seams.

3. Measure length of quilt. Trim blue borders to size and add to opposite sides of quilt

Quilt by Linda Winter

top. Press seam allowance toward borders. Measure width of quilt, including borders. Trim remaining 2 borders to size. Join to top and bottom of quilt.

4. Measure, trim, and add pink border to quilt.

Quilting and Finishing

1. Divide backing fabric into 3 (3-yard) lengths. Join along lengths to make backing.

2. Layer backing, batting, and quilt top; baste. Quilt as desired. Quilt shown was outline-quilted inside each cross and star piece, and background was filled with a diagonal grid pattern.

3. Join 2¼"-wide pink strips into 1 continuous piece for straight-grain French-fold binding. Add binding to quilt.

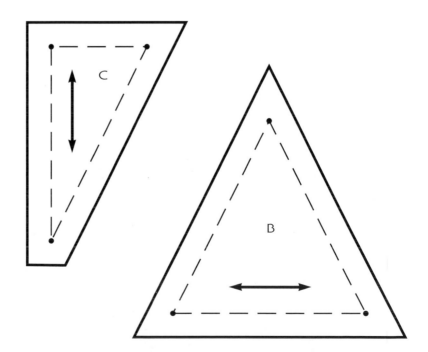

Flower Power

"I named this quilt Flower Power because the posy shape I drew reminds me of the pink and orange flower decals I had on my VW Bug back in 1969," says Marianne Fons. "Just for fun, I stitched rainbow rickrack over the sashing seams to give this quilt extra punch."

Finished Size: 75" x 92"
Blocks: 20 (14") Flower Blocks

Materials
4¼ yards light plaid for block backgrounds
10 assorted fat quarters plaids for pots, flowers, and stars
⅛ yard yellow plaid for flower and star centers
¼ yard each of 3 assorted green plaids for leaves and stems
4 yards bright stripe for sashing, borders, and binding
5½ yards backing
Full-size batting
14 (2½-yard) packages jumbo rick-rack (Wright's 001 Rainbow)
Template material or paper-backed fusible web
Freezer paper
Tailor's chalk
*Fat quarter = 18" x 22"

Cutting
Measurements include ¼" seam allowances. Cut crosswise strips unless otherwise noted. Border strips are exact length needed. You may want to cut them longer to allow for piecing variations. Patterns are on pages 36–38.

From light plaid, cut:
• 10 (14½"-wide) strips. Cut strips into 20 (14½") squares for block backgrounds.
• 1 (3½"-wide) strip. Cut strip into 12 (3½") sashing squares.

From 10 assorted plaids, cut:
• 2 flower pots per fabric.
• 6 flowers per fabric.
• 12 assorted stars.

From yellow plaid, cut:
• 72 circles for flower and star centers.

From 3 assorted green plaids, cut:
• 40 assorted leaves.
• 230" total of assorted 1⅛"-wide bias. Fold in thirds and press to make ⅜"-wide bias strips for stems. Cut into 40 (3") sections and 20 (5½") sections.

From bright stripe, cut:
• 8 (5½"-wide) strips. Match stripes and piece to make 2

(5½" x 82½") side borders and 2 (5½" x 75½") top and bottom borders.
• 16 (3½"-wide) strips. Cut strips into 31 (3½" x 14½") sashing strips.
• 1 (36") square for bias binding.

Block Assembly
1. On 1 (14½") light plaid background square, appliqué pieces in the following order using a buttonhole stitch: 3 bias stems (2 short and 1 long) in 3 fabrics, 2 leaves in fabrics to match bias, 3 different flowers, 3 flower centers, and 1 flower pot. (Refer to photo on page 39.)
2. Make 20 Flower blocks.
3. Appliqué 1 star and 1 circle on 1 (3½") light plaid sashing square using buttonhole stitch.
4. Make 12 sashing squares.

Quilt Assembly
1. Referring to *Block Row Diagram*, join 4 Flower blocks and 3 sashing strips into a row, alternating as shown. Make 5 block rows.

Block Row Diagram

2. Cut 1 (6") square from freezer paper. Use *Corner Scallop Pattern* on page 36 to cut 1 corner arc. Press to 1 corner, aligning with border scallops. Mark with chalk. Repeat for each corner. Do not trim yet.

3. Divide backing fabric into 2 (2¾-yard) lengths. Cut 1 piece in half lengthwise. Sew 1 narrow panel to each side of wide panel. Press seam allowances toward narrow panels.

4. Layer backing, batting, and quilt top; baste. Quilt as desired. Quilt shown was outline-quilted around appliqué shapes, and background of each block is filled with an interlocking wave pattern. Each pot has rows of small scallops. Sashing has 2 rows of wave stitching through center, and border is quilted in an echoing scallop pattern.

5. Make 12 yards of 2¼"-wide French-fold bias binding from bright stripe. Align raw edges of binding with chalk lines and stitch. When stitching is complete, trim excess quilt along curves. Turn binding to back of quilt and finish by hand.

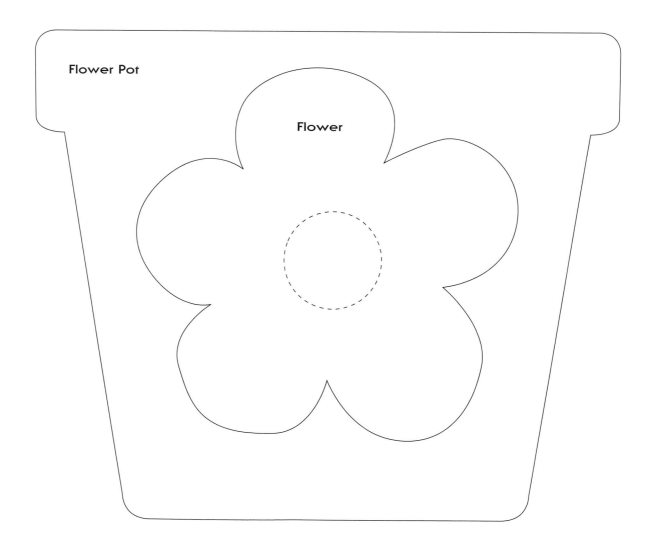

Flower Pot

Flower

Quilt by Marianne Fons; quilted by Lynn Witzenburg

Spinning Wheels

Traditional Winding Ways blocks create circles and curves in this quilt. Patricia Mullett appliquéd the pieces onto a background square rather than trying to piece those sharp curves. We've included templates with a seam allowance so you can choose the method you prefer.

Finished Size: 53" x 70"
Blocks: 35 (8½") Winding Ways Blocks

Materials
18 fat quarters* assorted dark plaids for blocks and border
18 fat quarters* assorted light plaids for blocks and border
½ yard light plaid for bias border
¾ yard brown plaid for border
¾ yard dark brown plaid for binding
3½ yards fabric for backing
Twin-size batting
Template material
*Fat quarter = 18" x 22"

Cutting
Measurements include ¼" seam allowances. Cutting below is for appliqué method. If you prefer to piece the blocks, see the tip box at right. Patterns are on page 42.

From assorted dark plaids, cut:
• 17 (9") squares for background.
• 18 sets of 4 matching As.

From assorted light plaids, cut:
• 18 (9") squares for background.
• 17 sets of 4 matching As.

From light plaid, cut:
• 1 (18") square. Use square to make 1¼"-wide continuous bias for bias borders. Make 2 (1¼" x 46") top and bottom bias borders and 2 (1¼" x 64½") side bias borders.

*B*ias stretches out of shape easily, so handle these borders carefully.—Liz

To make straight-grain borders, cut 6 crosswise strips. Piece to achieve needed length.

From brown plaid, cut:
• 6 (3½"-wide) strips. Piece to make 2 (3½" x 47½") top and bottom outer borders and 2 (3½" x 70½") side outer borders.

From dark brown plaid, cut:
• 7 (2¼"-wide) strips for binding.

From all assorted plaids, cut:
• 25–30 (2"-wide) random length (3"–14") sections for pieced border. Piece to make 2 (2" x 43") top and bottom borders and 2 (2" x 63") side borders.

Block Assembly
Appliqué dark As to light background squares to complete 18 blocks as shown in *Block Diagram*. Then make 17 blocks with light As on dark background squares. →

Piecing Instructions
If you prefer piecing blocks, follow these instructions for block assembly. Note that our staff rates this quilt as "challenging" if you choose to piece the block.

From assorted dark plaids, cut:
• 18 sets of 4 As.
• 17 sets of 4 Bs and 4 Cs.

From assorted light plaids, cut:
• 17 sets of 4 As.
• 18 sets of 4 Bs and 4 Cs.

1. Choose 1 dark A set and 1 set of matching light B and C pieces. Join 1 A to 1 B as shown in *Block Assembly Diagram*. Repeat to make 4 units.
2. Join 4 A/B units with 4 Cs as shown to complete block (*Block Diagram*). Make 18 blocks with dark As on light backgrounds and 17 blocks with light As on dark backgrounds.

Quilt Assembly

1. Referring to photo on facing page, lay out blocks in 7 horizontal rows of 5 blocks each, alternating dark and light blocks. Join into rows; join rows to complete center.

2. Add 43"-long pieced border to top and bottom of quilt. Add 63"-long pieced borders to quilt sides.

3. Add bias borders and outer borders in same manner.

Quilting and Finishing

1. Divide backing fabric into 2 (1¾-yard) lengths. Join long sides to make backing. Seam will be horizontal.

2. Layer backing, batting, and quilt top; baste. Quilt as desired. Quilt shown was outline-quilted in circles.

3. Join 2¼"-wide dark brown plaid strips into 1 continuous piece for straight-grain French-fold binding. Add binding to quilt.

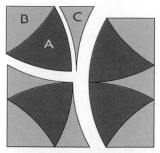

Block Assembly Diagram

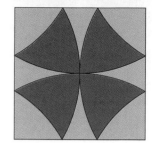

Block Diagram

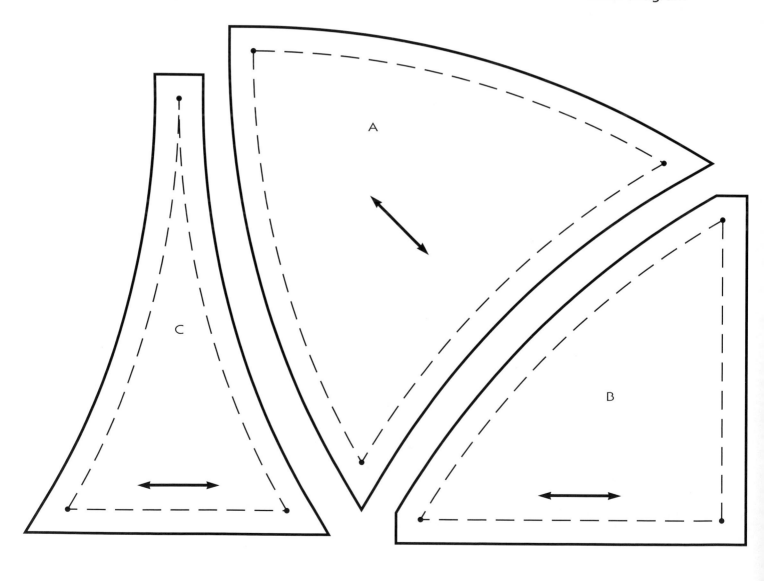

Quilt by Patricia Mullett

44

Kansas Troubles

This quilt pattern gets its name from a period before the Civil War when the Kansas-Nebraska Act was passed. The act required new states to hold a vote to decide whether they would become free or slave states. Abolitionist John Brown came to Kansas to campaign for the free-state cause. Fighting broke out over the issue and continued into the Civil War.

Finished Size: 84" x 100"
Blocks: 20 (16") Kansas Troubles Blocks, 40 (8") Evening Star Blocks

Materials
½ yard each 20 assorted dark prints
20 fat quarters* assorted light prints
¾ yard green print for binding
7½ yards fabric for backing
Queen-size batting
*Fat quarter = 18" x 22"

Cutting
Measurements include ¼" seam allowances. Cut cross-wise strips unless otherwise noted.

From each dark print, cut:
• 2 (8⅞") squares. Cut squares in half diagonally to make 4 half-square triangles (D).
• 2 (4⅞") squares. Cut squares in half diagonally to make 4 half-square triangles (C).
• 12 (2⅞") squares. Cut squares in half diagonally to make 24 half-square triangles (A).
• 2 (4½") squares (H) for star border.
• 16 (2½") squares (F) for star border.

From each light print, cut:
• 4 (2½") squares (B).
• 8 (2⅞") squares. Cut squares in half diagonally to make 16 half-square triangles (A).
• 8 (2½") squares (G) for stars.
• 8 (2½" x 4½") rectangles (E) for stars.
• 2 (2½" x 8½") spacer strips for stars.

From remaining light prints, cut:
• 4 (2½" x 10½") rectangles for border corner strips.

From green print, cut:
• 10 (2¼"-wide) strips for binding.

Kansas Troubles Block Assembly
1. Join 1 dark A triangle to 1 light A triangle (*A Unit Diagram*). Make 4 A Units.
2. Referring to *Kansas Troubles Unit Assembly Diagram*, lay out 4 A units, 2 dark A triangles, 1 B, 1 C, and 1 D, choosing colors as desired. Join into segments as shown. Join segments to complete unit.
3. Make 80 units. Join 4 units to complete block as shown in

Kansas Troubles Block Diagram.
4. Make 20 Kansas Troubles blocks. ➝

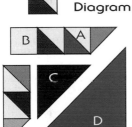

A Unit Diagram

Kansas Troubles Unit Assembly Diagram

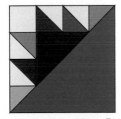

Kansas Troubles Unit Diagram

Kansas Troubles Block Diagram

Evening Star Block Assembly

1. Using diagonal-seams method, place 1 dark F atop 1 light E. Stitch diagonally as shown in *Diagonal Seams Diagrams*. Trim excess. Press back to reveal triangle. Repeat at other end as shown. Make 4 matching units.

2. Lay out 4 E/F units, 4 Gs, and 1 H, matching colors as shown in *Evening Star Block Assembly Diagram*. Join into rows; join rows. Add 1 (2½" x 8½") matching spacer strip to 1 side as shown in *Evening Star Block Diagram*.

3. Make 40 Evening Star blocks. Choose 4 blocks with light backgrounds that match remaining 4 (2½" x 10½") rectangles. Reserve these blocks for ends of top and bottom borders.

Border Assembly

1. Referring to *Quilt Top Assembly Diagram*, join 10 star blocks, alternating position of spacer strips as shown. Repeat to make 2 side borders.

2. Join 8 stars for top border, alternating position of the spacer strips. Place 1 end star on each end of strip. Add matching 2½" x 10½" rectangle to each end to complete. Repeat for bottom border.

Quilt Assembly

1. Arrange blocks in 5 horizontal rows of 4 blocks each. Join blocks into rows; join rows to complete center.

2. Join 1 (10-star) border to each side of quilt. Join top and bottom borders to quilt.

Quilting and Finishing

1. Divide backing fabric into 3 (2½-yard) lengths. Join along long sides to make backing. Seams will run parallel to top and bottom of quilt.

2. Layer backing, batting, and quilt top; baste. Quilt as desired. Quilt shown was machine-quilted.

3. Join 2¼"-wide green strips into 1 continuous piece for straight-grain French-fold binding. Add binding to quilt.

Diagonal Seams Diagrams

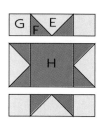

Evening Star Block Assembly Diagram

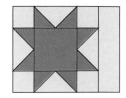

Evening Star Block Diagram

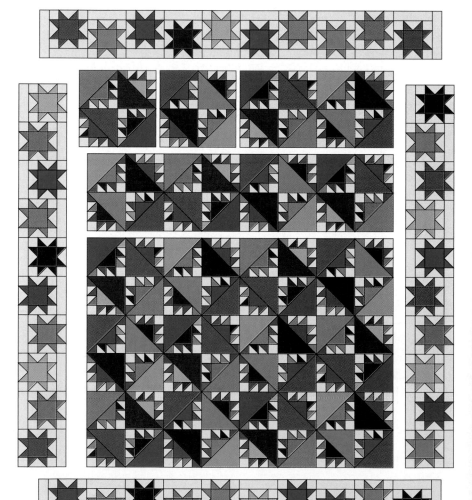

Quilt Top Assembly Diagram

Quilt designed by Lynn Rice, pieced by Marge Papuga, quilted by Theresa Schultz

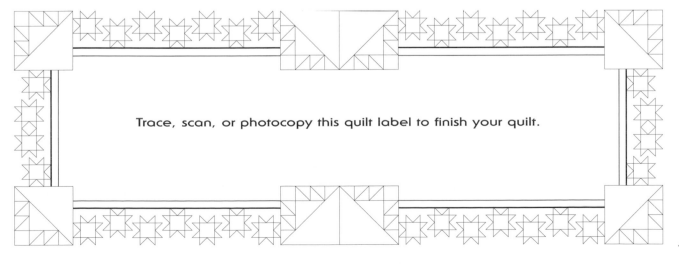

Trace, scan, or photocopy this quilt label to finish your quilt.

Rocky Mountain Puzzle

Although this quilt looks like an antique, quiltmaker Marion Roach Watchinski actually used current reproduction prints to give her project an old-time feel. The pattern dates back to 1933. This is an ideal quilt to showcase a collection of fat quarters.

Finished Size: 84" x 100"
Blocks: 72 (9") Rocky
Mountain Puzzle Blocks

Materials
36 fat quarters* (or 9 yards total) assorted dark prints for blocks
24 fat quarters* (or 6 yards total) assorted light prints for blocks
¾ yard pink print for border (3 yards for unpieced borders)
¾ yard brown print for binding
7½ yards backing
Queen size batting
*Fat quarter = 18" x 22"

Cutting
Measurements include ¼" seam allowances. Border strips are exact length needed. You may want to cut them longer to allow for piecing variations.

From each dark fat quarter, cut:
• 4 (2¾" x 9½") rectangles for a total of 120 sashing strips.
• 2 sets of:
  • 2 (1½" x 3") rectangles (B).
  • 2 (1½" x 5") rectangles (C).
  • 5 (3⅛") squares. Cut squares in half diagonally to make 10 half-square triangles (D).

From each light fat quarter, cut:
• 3 (2¾") squares for a total of 71 sashing squares.
• 3 sets of:
  • 1 (3") square (A).
  • 5 (3⅛") squares. Cut squares in half diagonally to make 10 half-square triangles (D).
  • 2 (2¾") squares (E).

From pink print, cut:
• 9 (2¾"-wide) strips. Piece to make 2 (2¾" x 80") top and bottom borders and 2 (2¾" x 100½") side borders (or trim to size after top is finished). If you prefer unpieced borders, cut 4 (2¾"-wide) lengthwise strips from alternate yardage.

From brown print, cut:
• 10 (2¼"-wide) strips for binding.

Block Assembly
Refer to *Block Assembly Diagram* throughout. Choose 1 light set and 1 dark set of pieces for each block.
1. Join 1 B to opposite sides of 1 A. Add 1 C to top and bottom of A/B unit (*A/B/C Unit Diagram*).
2. Join 1 light and 1 dark D to make a half-square triangle (*Half-square Diagram*). Make 10

D half-square units.
3. Join 2 D units as shown. Repeat. Add to sides of block. Join 3 D units and 1 E square into a strip. Repeat. Add to top and bottom of block (*Block Diagram*).
4. Make 72 blocks. ➡

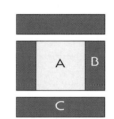
A/B/C Unit Diagram

Half-square Diagram

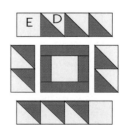
Block Assembly Diagram

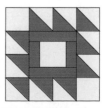
Block Diagram

Quilt Assembly

1. Lay out blocks, sashing strips, and sashing squares as shown in *Quilt Top Assembly Diagram*. Join into diagonal rows; join rows to complete top. Trim excess blocks from edges, leaving ¼" seam allowance.

2. Measure width of quilt. Trim shorter pink print borders to size and add to top and bottom of quilt top. Press seam allowance toward borders. Measure length of quilt, including borders. Trim remaining 2 borders to size. Join to sides of quilt.

Quilting and Finishing

1. Divide backing fabric into 3 (2½-yard) lengths. Join along long sides to make backing. Seams will run horizontally.

2. Layer backing, batting, and quilt top; baste. Quilt as desired. Quilt shown was hand-quilted in Baptist Fans.

3. Join 2¼"-wide brown print strips into 1 continuous piece for straight-grain French-fold binding. Add binding to quilt.

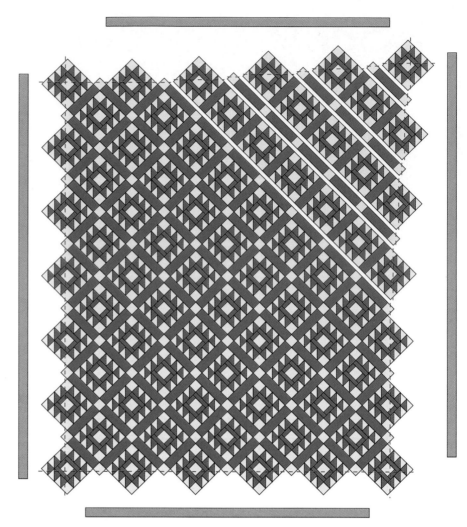

Quilt Top Assembly Diagram

Trace, scan, or photocopy this quilt label to finish your quilt.

Quilt by Marion Roach Watchinski

Wild Goose Chase

Carole Collins enjoys making multi-fabric quilts that look like antiques. "I chose to make Wild Goose Chase into a small quilt so that it would fit on our antique rope bed and still allow the ropes to be seen." The traditional color scheme makes this quilt an ideal accent piece.

Finished Size: 63¾" x 76½"
**Blocks: 30 (12¾") Wild
Goose Chase Blocks**

Materials
13 fat quarters* dark blue prints
3 fat quarters* dark gold prints
15 fat quarters* assorted light
   shirting prints and plaids
15 fat quarters* assorted dark
   red prints, plaids, and stripes
¾ yard plaid fabric for binding
4 yards fabric for backing
Twin-size batting
*Fat quarter = 18" x 22"

Cutting
Measurements include ¼" seam allowances. Cut crosswise strips unless otherwise noted.

From each dark blue and dark gold fat quarter, cut:
• 3 (3½"-wide) strips. Cut strips into:
   • 24 (2" x 3½") rectangles (B).

• 2 (3½") squares (E).
• 2 (2⅝"-wide) strips. Cut strips into 8 (2⅝") squares (D). (You will have 1 extra set of blue and gold.)

From each light fat quarter, cut:
• 5 (2"-wide) strips. Cut strips into 48 (2") squares (A).
• 1 (2⅜"-wide) strip. Cut strip into 8 (2⅜") squares. Cut squares in half diagonally to make 16 C triangles.

From each red fat quarter, cut:
• 2 (9¾") squares. Cut squares in quarters diagonally to make 8 F triangles.

From plaid, cut:
• 1 (29") square for bias binding.

Block Assembly
1. Choose 1 set each of dark, light, and red prints.

2. Referring to *Diagonal Seams Diagrams*, lay 1 A atop 1 end of B. Using diagonal seams, stitch diagonally as shown. Trim excess and open out. Lay 1 A atop opposite end of B and stitch. Trim and open out. Make 12 matching Goose Chase Units.
3. Join 1 C triangle to 1 side of 1 D square as shown in Diagram 1. Repeat on adjacent side. Make 4 matching Corner Units.
4. Join 3 Goose Chase Units and 1 Corner Unit as shown in *Diagram 2*. Make 4 pieced units.
5. Referring to *Block Assembly Diagram*, join 2 pieced units to opposite sides of 1 E square. Join 1 F triangle to each side of remaining pieced units. Join to complete block (*Block Diagram*).
6. Make 25 blue and 5 gold Wild Goose Chase blocks. ➤

Diagonal Seams Diagrams

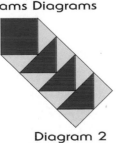

Diagram 1

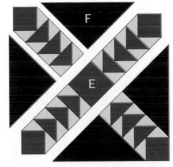

Diagram 2   **Block Assembly Diagram**

Block Diagram

Quilt Assembly

1. Lay out blocks in 6 horizontal rows of 5 blocks each.

2. Join into rows; join rows to complete top.

Quilting and Finishing

1. Divide backing fabric into 2 (2-yard) lengths. Cut 1 piece in half lengthwise. Sew 1 narrow panel to each side of wide panel. Press seam allowances toward narrow panels. Seams will run horizontally.

2. Layer backing, batting, and quilt top; baste. Quilt as desired. Quilt shown was quilted in-the-ditch around leading edge of each goose, and red backgrounds were quilted in parallel lines.

3. Make bias binding from 29" plaid square. Add binding to quilt.

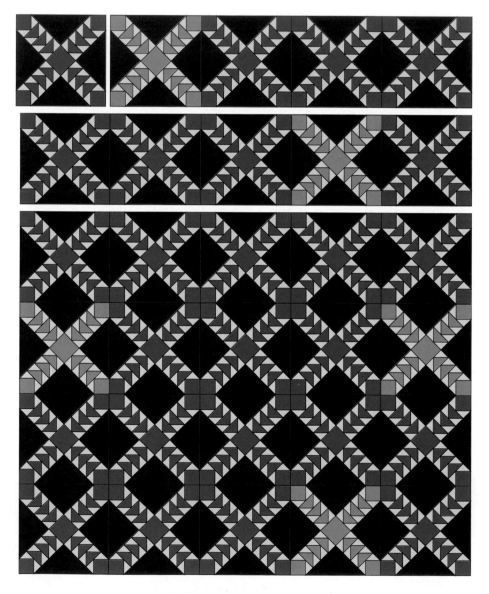

Quilt Top Assembly Diagram

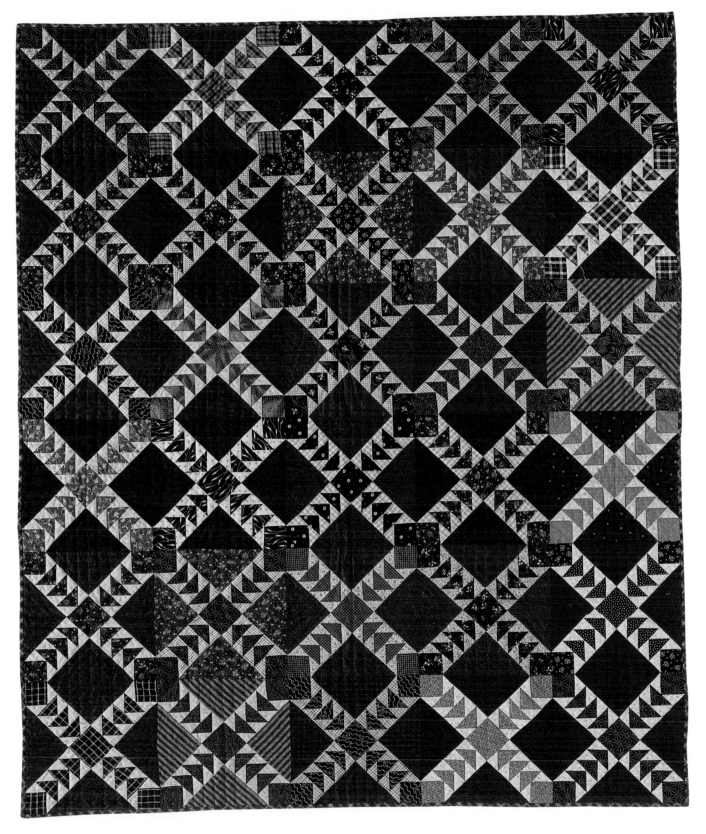

Quilt by Carole Collins

Circle Safari

"Marianne and I had a nice collection of African print fabrics we wanted to play with," says Liz Porter. "Because the prints were big, we wanted to keep our patchwork shapes large, too. The larger shapes made the curved seams easy to handle. After we made the units, we experimented with ways to set them together."

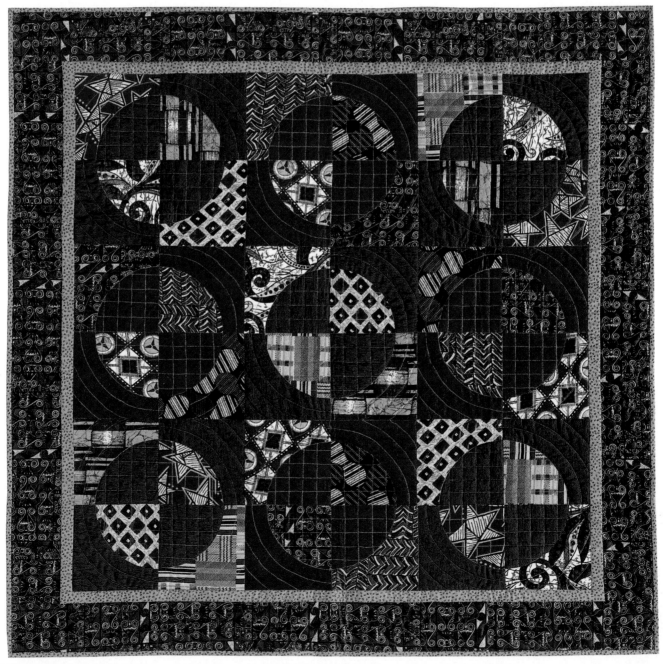

Finished Size: 52" x 52"
Blocks: 9 (14") Drunkard's
Path Blocks

Materials
8 fat eighths* exotic medium-
  to large-scale prints for
  blocks
1 yard dark red print for blocks
1 yard dark green print for
  blocks
1½ yards dark exotic print for
  blocks and border
¾ yard orange print for inner
  border and binding
3½ yards exotic print for backing, or 1¾ yards 60"-wide
  fabric
60" x 60" scrap batting
Freezer paper
*Fat eighth = 9" x 22"

Cutting
Measurements include ¼"
seam allowances. Cut crosswise strips unless otherwise
noted. See instructions below
to make freezer-paper templates for patterns A and B on
pages 58–59.

From freezer paper, cut:
• 1 A (quarter circle) pattern
  piece.
• 1 B (background) pattern
  piece. Fold exotic prints,
  dark red, and dark green fabrics in half, press shiny side
  of freezer-paper templates
  onto fabric, and use scissors
  or small rotary cutter to cut
  fabric pieces. Peel freezer-
  paper templates from fabric
  pieces and reuse; make new
  templates when originals will
  no longer adhere to fabric.
  Cut the following fabric
  pieces:

From each exotic print, cut:
• 2 As (for a total of 18).
• 2 Bs (for a total of 18).

From dark red print, cut:
• 8 As.
• 8 Bs.

From dark green print, cut:
• 10 As.
• 10 Bs.

From dark exotic print, cut:
• 4 (4½"-wide) lengthwise
  strips. Cut strips into 2 (4½"
  x 44½") top and bottom
  outer borders. Cut 2 (4½" x
  52½") side outer borders.
  Use remainder to cut additional As and Bs.

From orange print, cut:
• 5 (1½"-wide) strips. Cut strips
  into 2 (1½" x 42½") top and
  bottom inner borders. Piece
  remaining strips to make
  2 (1½" x 44½") side inner
  borders.
• 6 (2¼"-wide) strips for
  straight-grain binding.

Unit Assembly
1. Fold each A piece in half
and finger-press to make a
small crease along outer
curved edge to mark center
curve. Repeat for each B
piece.
2. Match each exotic print A
with either a red or green B.
Match each exotic print B with
either a red or green A.
3. With right sides facing and
B on top, match center creases and ends and pin. Stitch
along curved edges, aligning
and smoothing as you go. Clip
seams and press seam
allowances toward A.
4. Make 36 units (*Unit
Diagram*).

Quilt Assembly
1. Referring to *Block
Assembly Diagram*, join 4
units as shown. Referring to
photo, make 5 green blocks
and 4 red blocks.
2. Referring to *Quilt Top
Assembly Diagram*, join
blocks into 3 horizontal rows
of 3 blocks each, alternating
as shown. Press seam
allowances in opposite directions in alternating rows. Join
rows to complete center of
quilt top.
3. Add 1 (1½" x 42½") orange
inner border to sides of quilt
top. Press seam allowances
toward borders. Add 1 (1½" x
44½") orange inner border to
top and bottom of quilt. Press
seam allowances toward
borders.
4. Add 1 (4½" x 44½") dark
outer border to quilt sides.
Press seam allowances
toward borders. Add 1 (4½" x
52½") dark outer border to top
and bottom of quilt. Press
seam allowances toward
borders. ➡

Unit Diagram

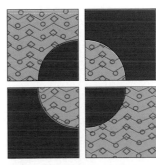

Block Assembly Diagram

Quilting and Finishing

1. Divide backing into 2 (1¾-yard) lengths. Cut 1 piece in half lengthwise. Sew 1 narrow panel to long side of wide panel. Press seam allowance toward narrow panel. Set aside extra panel for hanging sleeve, if desired.

2. Layer backing, batting, and quilt top; baste. Quilt as desired. Liz machine-quilted a grid pattern in the A pieces and an arc pattern in the B pieces. She used a meandering quilting pattern in the borders.

3. Join 2¼"-wide orange strips into 1 continuous piece for French-fold straight-grain binding. Add binding to quilt.

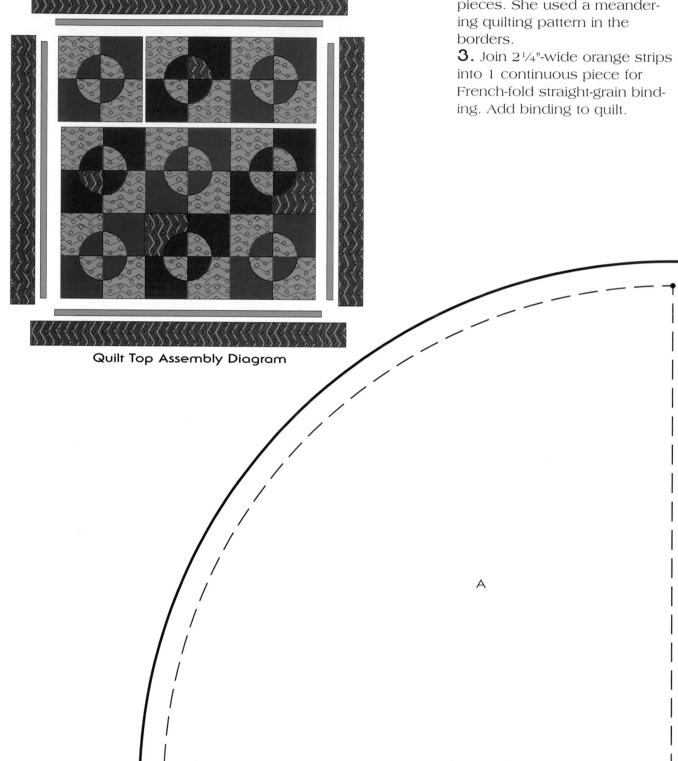

Quilt Top Assembly Diagram

A

B

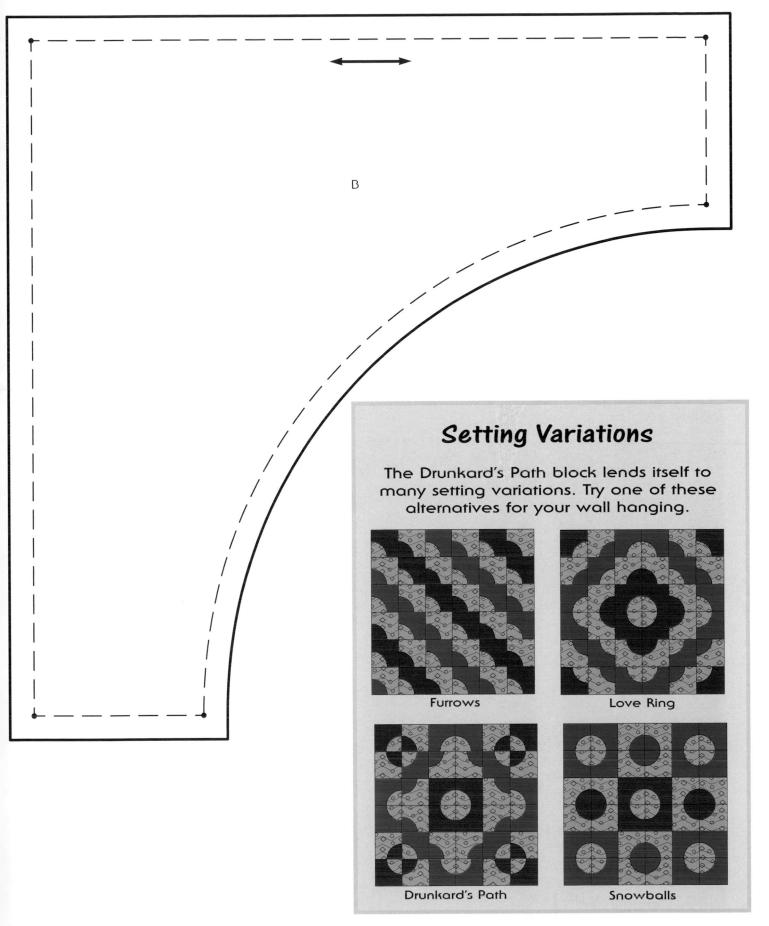

Setting Variations

The Drunkard's Path block lends itself to many setting variations. Try one of these alternatives for your wall hanging.

Furrows

Love Ring

Drunkard's Path

Snowballs

Liz's Plaid Stars

Feature your favorite plaids in this design by Liz Porter. The zigzag border creates a frame for the playful stars.

Finished Size: 32" x 32"
Blocks: 9 (8") Variable Star Blocks

Materials
18 fat eighths* or scraps assorted medium and dark plaids
9 fat eighths* or scraps assorted light plaids
1 yard fabric for backing
3/8 yard multicolored plaid for binding
40" x 40" piece of batting
*Fat eighth = 9" x 22"

Cutting
Measurements include 1/4" seam allowances. Cut crosswise strips unless otherwise noted.

From medium and dark plaids, cut:
• 9 sets of star points. For each set, cut 8 (2½") matching squares (B).
• 52 (2½" x 4½") assorted rectangles for border triangles.
• 8 (2½") assorted squares for border end triangles and border squares.
• 9 (4½") assorted squares for star centers (A).

From light plaids, cut:
• 9 sets of star backgrounds. For each set, cut 4 (2½") squares (D) and 4 (2½" x 4½") rectangles (C).

• 48 (2½" x 4½") assorted rectangles for border triangles.
• 12 (2½") assorted squares for border end triangles.

From multicolored plaid, cut:
• 4 (2¼"-wide) strips for binding.

Block Assembly
1. Referring to *Diagonal Seams Diagrams*, lay 1 B atop 1 end of 1 C, with right sides facing. Stitch diagonally as shown. Trim excess and press open. Repeat on opposite end to make 1 Goose Chase unit. Make 4 matching Goose Chase units.

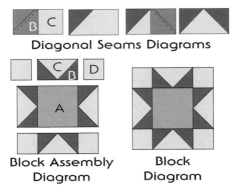

Diagonal Seams Diagrams

Block Assembly Diagram

Block Diagram

2. Lay out 1 A, 4 matching Goose Chase units, and 4 matching Ds as shown in *Block Assembly Diagram*.
3. Join into rows; join rows to complete block (*Block Diagram*).
4. Make 9 blocks.

Border Assembly
1. Using diagonal seams and referring to *Border Assembly Diagrams*, make strips of triangles for inner borders. Lay 1 light rectangle atop 1 dark rectangle, with right sides facing, and stitch diagonally as shown. Trim excess and press open. Repeat, alternating dark and light rectangles. Make 2 (6 dark, 5 light) strips and 2 (6 dark, 7 light) strips for inner borders.
2. Using diagonal seams and referring to *Border Finishing Diagram*, lay 1 (2½") light square atop 1 end of shorter inner border strip. Stitch ➡

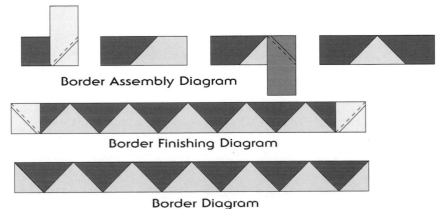

Border Assembly Diagram

Border Finishing Diagram

Border Diagram

diagonally as shown. Trim and press open. Repeat at other end (*Border Diagram*). Add light squares to ends of shorter borders and dark squares to ends of longer borders.

3. Make 4 (7 dark, 6 light, 2 light square) strips for outer border. Finish ends with light squares.

Quilt Assembly

1. Arrange blocks in 3 hori-zontal rows of 3 blocks each, as shown in *Quilt Top Assembly Diagram*. Join into rows; join rows.

2. Referring to *Quilt Top Assembly Diagram*, join 1 shorter inner border strip to each side of quilt. Join remaining inner border strips to top and bottom.

3. Join 1 outer border strip to each side of quilt. Add 1 (2½") dark square to each end of remaining strips. Add to top and bottom of quilt.

Quilting and Finishing

1. Layer backing, batting, and quilt top; baste. Quilt as desired. Quilt shown was utility-quilted. Border is outline-quilted.

2. Join 2¼"-wide multicolored plaid strips into 1 continuous piece for straight-grain French-fold binding. Add binding.

Quilt Top Assembly Diagram

Quilt by Liz Porter

Homespun Pleasures

When Mary Gray Hart made this quilt, she had no idea it would be hanging at the American Quilters' Society show in Paducah, Kentucky, the following year. Use your collection of plaids to make your own cozy nap-size quilt.

Finished Size: 59½" x 74½"
Blocks: 18 (7½") 54-40 or Fight Blocks, 17 (7½") Courthouse Steps Blocks

Materials
12-20 fat eighths* or fat quarters** assorted light plaids and prints (1¾ yards total) for blocks
12-20 fat eighths* or fat quarters** assorted dark plaids and prints (2¼ yards total) for blocks and inner border
4-6 assorted dark red prints (1½ yards total) for border and binding
4-6 assorted dark plaids (1½ yards total) for borders
3½ yards fabric for backing
Template plastic
Pearl cotton for utility quilting (optional)
*Fat eighth = 9" x 22"
**Fat quarter = 18" x 22"

Cutting
Most blocks have matched fabrics in them. Some are mixed for a scrappier look. Make templates using patterns A and B on page 67. Cutting instructions are for matched blocks, but you may substitute as desired. Measurements include ¼" seam allowances. Cut crosswise strips unless otherwise noted. Border strips are exact length needed; you may want to cut them longer to allow for piecing variations.

From assorted light plaids and prints, cut:
• 11 (1½" x 22") assorted strips for Courthouse Steps. From these, cut:
• 17 sets of 2 matching 1½" x 2" rectangles.
• 17 sets of 2 matching 1½" x 4" rectangles.
• 17 sets of 2 matching 1½" x 6" rectangles.
• 12 sets of 4 matching As for dark star blocks.
• 12 sets of 4 matching 3" squares (C) for dark star blocks.
• 6 sets of 4 matching Bs and B rev. to make 8 matching points for light star blocks.
• 6 (3") squares (C) to match B point sets for light star centers.
• 4 different 3" squares for inner border corners.

From assorted dark plaids and prints, cut:
• 16 (1½" x 22") assorted strips for Courthouse Steps. From these, cut:
• 17 sets of 2 matching 1½" x 4" rectangles.
• 17 sets of 2 matching 1½" x 6" rectangles.
• 17 sets of 2 matching 1½" x 8" rectangles.
• 5 (3"-wide) assorted strips. Cut strips into random lengths from 10" to 22". Piece to make 2 (3" x 53") inner side borders and 2 (3" x 38") inner top and bottom borders.
• 6 sets of 4 matching As for light star blocks.
• 12 sets of 4 matching Bs and B rev. to make 8 matching points for dark star blocks.
• 12 (3") squares to match B point sets for dark star centers.

From dark red prints, cut:
• 17 assorted 2" squares for Courthouse Steps centers.
• 6 (1½"-wide) assorted strips. Cut strips into random lengths from 12" to 30". Piece to make 2 (1½" x 58") middle side borders and 2 (1½" x 45") middle top and bottom borders.
• 7 (2¼"-wide) assorted strips for straight-grain binding.

From dark plaids, cut:
• 7 (8"-wide) assorted strips. Piece to make 2 (8" x 75") outside borders and 2 (8" x 45") outer top and bottom borders. ➡

54-40 or Fight Block Assembly

1. Join 1 dark B and 1 matching dark B rev. to each side of 1 light A. Make 4 matching units.

2. Lay out 4 matching A/B units, 1 matching dark C, and 4 matching light Cs as shown in *54-40 or Fight Block Assembly Diagram.* Press seam allowances toward C squares. Join into rows; join rows to complete a dark star with a light background.

3. Referring to *Block Diagrams,* make 12 dark stars with light backgrounds and 6 light stars with dark backgrounds.

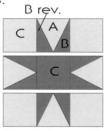

54-40 Fight Block Assembly Diagram

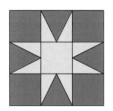 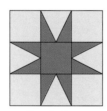

Light Star Block Diagram   **Dark Star Block Diagram**

Courthouse Steps Block Assembly

1. Join 1 set of light 1½" x 2" rectangles to opposite sides of 1 (2") red square. Press seam allowances away from center square. Join 1 set of dark 1½" x 4" rectangles to opposite sides of this unit. Referring to *Courthouse Steps Block Assembly Diagram,* continue with increasing set lengths, alternating light and dark sets,

and stopping with third set of rectangles. Press seam allowances away from center.

2. Make 17 Courthouse Steps blocks, as shown in *Courthouse Steps Block Assembly Diagram.*

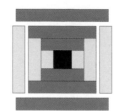 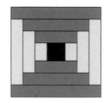

Courthouse Steps Block Assembly Diagram   **Courthouse Steps Block Diagram**

Quilt Top Assembly

1. Join 3 dark star blocks as shown in *Row A Assembly Diagram.* Make 4 of Row A. Press seam allowances toward star blocks.

2. Join 3 Courthouse Steps blocks and 2 light star blocks as shown in *Row A Assembly Diagram.* Press seam allowances toward star blocks. Make 3 of row B.

3. Referring to photo, join rows to complete the quilt center.

4. Join 3" x 53" inner borders to each side of quilt. Press

seam allowances towards borders. Join 1 (3") light square to each end of 3" x 38" top and bottom borders. Add borders to quilt, matching seams. Press as before.

5. Add 1 (1½" x 58") red border to each side of quilt. Add 1 (1½" x 45") red border to quilt top and bottom.

6. Add 8" x 45" plaid borders to top and bottom of quilt. Add 8" x 75" plaid border to each side of quilt.

Quilting and Finishing

1. Divide backing fabric into 2 (1¾-yard) lengths. Cut 1 piece in half lengthwise. Sew 1 narrow panel to each side of wide panel. Press seam allowances toward narrow panels. Seams on backing will run parallel to top and bottom of quilt top.

2. Layer backing batting, and quilt top; baste. Quilt as desired. Quilt shown is utility-quilted with pearl cotton in an overall clamshell design.

3. Join 2¼"-wide assorted red strips into 1 continuous piece to make approximately 8 yards of French-fold straight-grain binding. Add binding to quilt.

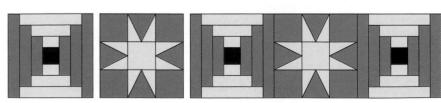

Row A Assembly Diagram

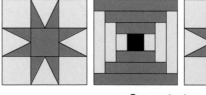

Row B Assembly Diagram

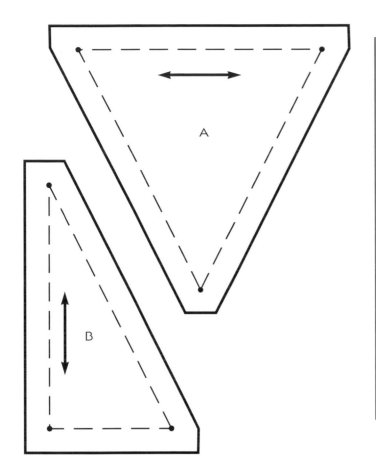

A

B

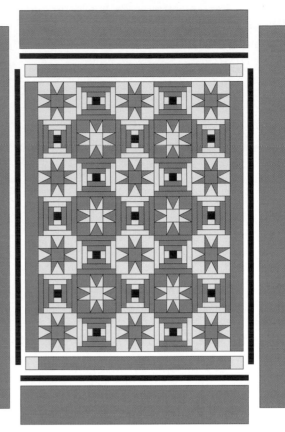

Quilt Top Assembly Diagram

Quilt by Mary Gray Hart

Safe Landing

Donna Larson made this quilt for her son Kurt. "He saw this Country Threads pattern and wanted it for his bed," says Donna. "I added a piped border and used leftovers from the airplanes to make an outer pieced border."

Finished Size: 63½" x 84½"
Blocks: 35 (8") Airplane Blocks

Materials
22 fat quarters* assorted blue prints for blocks, sashing strips, and border
2¼ yards white-on-white star print for block background
½ yard total assorted red prints for sashing blocks (or 48 (2⅛" x 4¼") assorted scraps)
¼ yard dark blue print for piping
¾ yard red print for binding
5 yards fabric for backing
Twin-size batting
*Fat quarter = 18" x 22"

Cutting
Measurements include ¼" seam allowances. Patterns are on page 70.

From each of 18 blue fat quarters, cut:
- 2 (1½" x 2½") rectangles (A).
- 2 (2½" x 8½") rectangles (C).
- 2 Ds.
- 4 (3" x 8½") sashing strips.
- 1 (4¾" x 11½") border rectangle.

From remaining 4 blue fat quarters, cut:
- 10 (3" x 8½") sashing strips.
- 8 (4¾" x 11½") border rectangles.

From white star print, cut:
- 5 (2⅛"-wide) strips. Cut strips into 96 (2⅛") squares. Cut squares in half diagonally to make 192 half-square triangles (F) for sashing blocks.
- 8 (1½"-wide) strips. Cut strips into 70 (1½" x 4½") rectangles (B).
- 35 Es.
- 35 E rev.

From assorted red prints, cut:
- 48 sets of 2 (2⅛") squares. Cut squares in half diagonally to make 48 sets of 4 half-square triangles (F) for sashing blocks.

From dark blue print, cut:
- 8 (¾"-wide) strips. Join in pairs end to end; fold in half with wrong sides facing and press to make 4 (⅜"-wide) lengths of piping.

From red print, cut:
- 8 (2¼"-wide) strips for binding.

Block Assembly
1. Choose 1 set of blue A/C/D pieces. Referring to *Diagonal Seams Diagrams*, lay 1 blue A atop 1 white B as shown. Stitch diagonally and trim excess. Repeat with 1 B on opposite side to complete A/B unit.
2. Set in 1 E to 1 D. Set in 1 E rev. to opposite side of D.
3. Join 1 A/B unit, 1 C, and 1 D/E unit as shown in *Airplane Block Assembly Diagram* to complete airplane block.
4. Make 35 Airplane blocks (*Airplane Block Diagram*). ➡

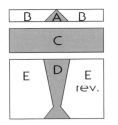

Airplane Block Assembly Diagram

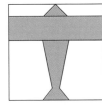

Airplane Block Diagram

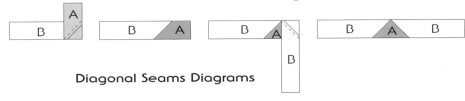

Diagonal Seams Diagrams

5. Join 1 red F triangle and 1 white F triangle as shown (*Triangle-Square Diagram*). Make 4 triangle-squares. Join as shown in *Pinwheel Block Assembly Diagram* to complete block (*Pinwheel Block Diagram*).

6. Make 48 Pinwheel blocks.

Quilt Assembly

1. Lay out airplane blocks in 7 rows of 5 blocks each. Refer to photo for orientation of airplanes from row to row. Alternate sashing strips between blocks; join to complete each row.

2. Join 6 Pinwheels and 5 sashing strips as shown in *Sashing Row Assembly Diagram*. Make 8 sashing rows.

3. Alternate sashing rows and block rows. Join to complete quilt top.

4. Measure length of quilt. Trim 2 lengths of piping to size. Baste in place along each side. Measure width of quilt. Trim remaining piping to size and baste in place along top and bottom edges.

5. Join blue border rectangles to make 2 (4¾" x 77") side bor-

Triangle-Square Diagram

Pinwheel Block Assembly Diagram

Pinwheel Block Diagram

Sashing Row Assembly Diagram

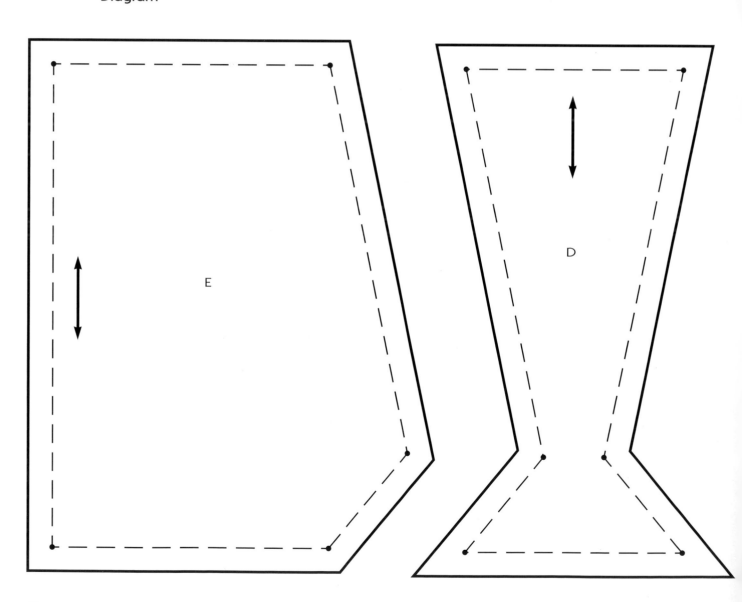

E

D

ders and 2 (4¾" x 66") top and bottom borders.

6. Measure length of quilt and trim 2 side borders to size. Join to quilt sides. Measure width of quilt (including borders) and trim remaining 2 borders to size. Join to top and bottom of quilt.

Quilting and Finishing

1. Divide backing fabric into 2 (2½-yard) lengths. Cut 1 piece in half lengthwise. Sew 1 narrow panel to each side of wide panel. Press seam allowances toward narrow panels.

2. Layer backing, batting, and quilt top; baste. Quilt as

desired. Quilt shown was row-quilted with a wave pattern that follows direction of planes. Border has a star pattern.

3. Join 2¼"-wide red print strips into 1 continuous piece for straight-grain French-fold binding. Add binding to quilt.

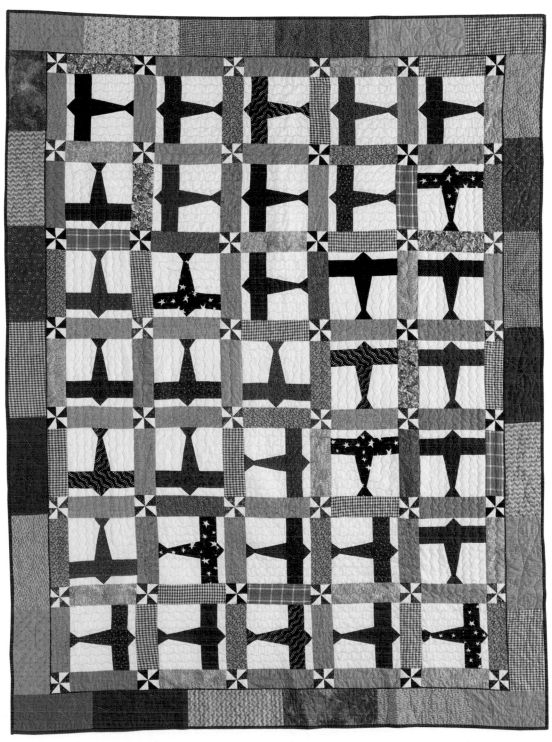

Quilt by Donna J. Larson, adapted from a pattern by Country Threads

Sunshine and Sunflowers

"Sunflowers' bright colors and in-your-face attitude make me smile," says Terri Shinn. "I designed this quilt with help from my friend George Taylor when I lived in Anchorage, Alaska. Every February, I craved yellow. I would fill my house with daffodils from the grocery store and work on a quilt with yellow in it."

Finished Size: 76" x 62"
Blocks: 12 (14") Sunflower
Blocks

Materials
12 fat eighths* assorted blue
   prints, light to dark, for block
   backgrounds
12 fat quarters** assorted gold
   prints for sunflowers
12 (7") squares assorted dark
   gold-and-brown prints for
   sunflower centers
1/3 yard each of 4 different
   green prints for leaves and
   vines
Scraps of 4–8 green prints for
   additional leaves
4 1/4 yards green-and-blue background print
1/2 yard green print for binding
4 yards fabric for backing
Twin-size batting
Template material
*Fat eighth = 9" x 22"
**Fat quarter = 18" x 22"

Cutting
Measurements include 1/4"
seam allowances. Cut crosswise
strips unless otherwise noted.
Patterns are on pages 74–75.

From each blue fat eighth, cut:
• 12 As.

From each gold fat quarter, cut:
• 12 Bs.

From assorted dark gold-and-
brown prints, cut:
• 12 Cs.

From assorted green prints,
cut:
• 1 (4 1/2" x 65") strip from each
   of 4 green prints, piecing as
   needed. These will become
   free-form vines for each
   border.

• 16 large leaves.
• 12 medium leaves.
• 11 small leaves.

From green-and-blue print, cut:
• 1 3/4 yards. From this, cut:
   • 2 (10 1/2" x 62 1/2") lengthwise
      strips for top and bottom
      borders.
   • 2 (10 1/2" x 42 1/2") lengthwise
      strips for side borders.
• 6 (14 1/2"-wide) strips. Cut
   strips into 12 (14 1/2") squares
   for flower background.

From green print, cut:
• 7 (2 1/4"-wide) strips for
   binding.

Block Assembly
1. Join 1 blue A to 1 gold B
as shown in *Piecing Diagram*.
Stop stitching exactly at
marked dots. Make 12 matching A/B units. Join units in a
circle. Appliqué 1 C circle in
center.
2. Center sunflower on 1
background square and
appliqué. Carefully snip away
background fabric behind
appliqué, leaving 1/4" seam
allowance.
3. Make 12 Sunflower Blocks
(*Block Diagram*).

Quilt Assembly
1. Lay out blocks in 3 horizontal rows of 4 blocks each.
Arrange so that blue sunflower
backgrounds range from light
to dark through rows. Join
blocks into rows; join rows.
2. Measure width of quilt. Join
10 1/2" x 42 1/2" borders to quilt
sides. Join 10 1/2" x 62 1/2" borders to quilt top and bottom.
Press seam allowance toward
borders.
3. From each of 4 (4 1/2" x 65")
green strips, trim fabric to form

vines, cutting vine 1/2" wider
than desired finished width for
seam allowance.
4. Using photo on page 74 as
a guide, appliqué 1 green vine
to each border, varying width
and curves as shown or as
desired. Appliqué leaves as
shown.

Quilting and Finishing
1. Divide backing fabric into 2
(2-yard) lengths. Cut 1 piece in
half lengthwise. Sew 1 narrow
panel to each side of wide
panel. Press seam allowances
toward narrow panels.
2. Layer backing, batting, and
quilt top; baste. Quilt as
desired. Quilt shown has veins
quilted into each petal and
leaf, and a grid pattern in each
flower center. Vines have a
wave pattern, and green-and-
blue background is grid quilted.
3. Join 2 1/4"-wide green print
strips into 1 continuous piece
for straight-grain French-fold
binding. Add binding to quilt.

Piecing Diagram

Block Diagram

Quilt by Terri Shinn

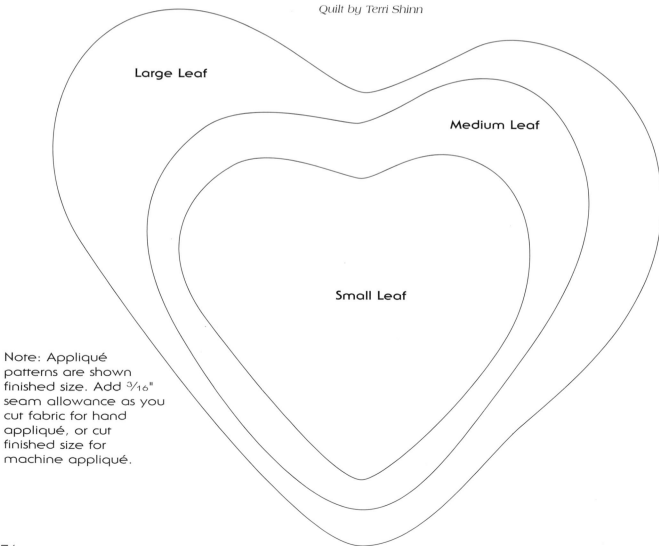

Large Leaf

Medium Leaf

Small Leaf

Note: Appliqué
patterns are shown
finished size. Add ³⁄₁₆"
seam allowance as you
cut fabric for hand
appliqué, or cut
finished size for
machine appliqué.

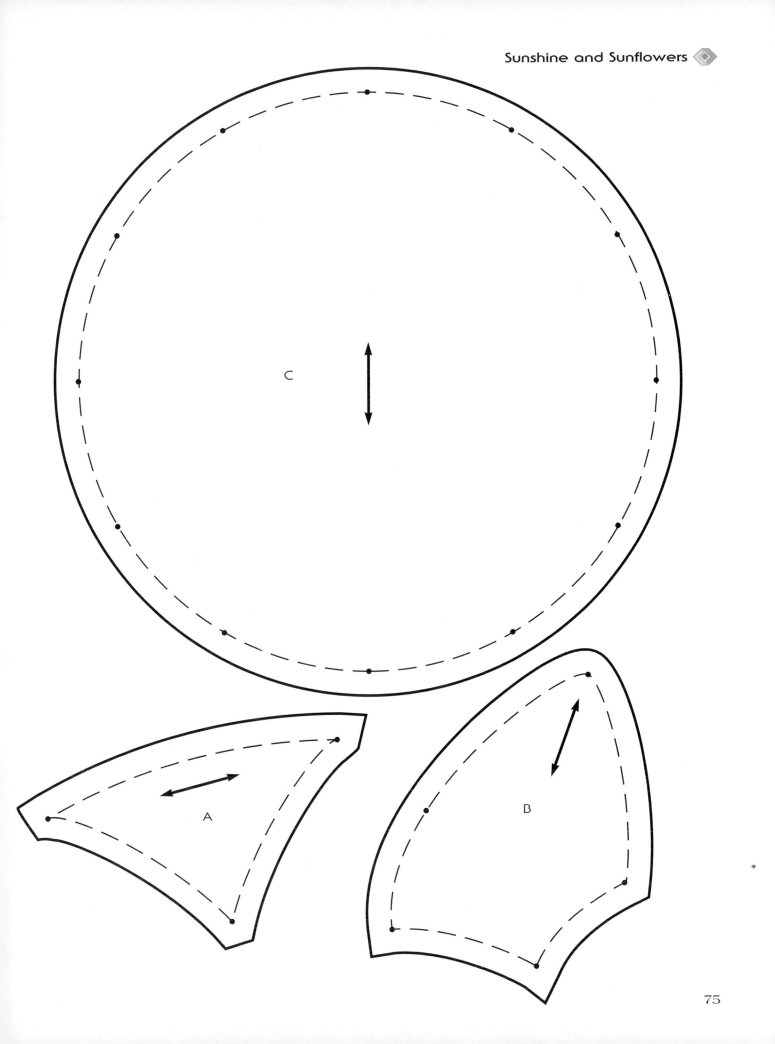

The House That Jack Built

"Several years ago, I visited Stoudt's Black Angus Antique Mall in Adamstown, Pennsylvania, in Lancaster County," says Connie Tilman. "While walking through the maze of booths, I spied a beautiful quilt that had green and double-pink calicoes characteristic of turn-of-the-century Lancaster quilts. Marianne and Liz had just given me pieces of their shirting fabrics, and I was searching for the right quilt pattern to showcase them. This old pattern was the perfect project."

Finished Size: 71" x 83"
Blocks: 30 (8½") Blocks

Materials
30 fat eighths* assorted dark prints for blocks
30 fat eighths* assorted light prints for blocks
1¾ yards dark green print for blocks
2½ yards first pink print for setting pieces
2¼ yards second pink print for unpieced borders or 1½ yards for pieced borders
5 yards light green print for backing
¾ yard medium green print for binding
Full-size batting
*Fat eighth = 9" x 22"

Cutting
Measurements include ¼" seam allowances. Cut crosswise strips unless otherwise noted. Border strips are exact length needed. You may want to cut them longer to allow for piecing variations.

From each dark print, cut:
• 1 (1½" x 22") strip for Rail Fence units, for a total of 30 strips.

From each light print, cut:
• 2 (1½" x 22") strips for Rail Fence units, for a total of 60 strips.

From dark green print, cut:
• 3 (3½"-wide) strips. Cut strips into 30 (3½") squares for block centers.
• 5 (5½"-wide) strips. Cut strips into 30 (5½") squares. Cut squares in quarters diagonally to make 120 side setting triangles for blocks.
• 5 (3"-wide) strips. Cut strips into 60 (3") squares. Cut squares in half diagonally to make 120 corner setting triangles for blocks.

From first pink print, cut:
• 5 (9"-wide) strips. Cut strips into 20 (9") squares for setting squares.
• 2 (13¼" wide) strips. Cut

strips into 5 (13¼") squares. Cut squares in quarters diagonally to make 20 side setting triangles. (You will have 2 extra.)
• 1 (7"-wide) strip. Cut strip into 2 (7") squares. Cut squares in half diagonally to make 4 corner setting triangles.

From second pink print:
If using 2¼ yards, cut:
• 4 (6"-wide) lengthwise strips. Cut 2 (6" x 72½") side borders and 2 (6" x 71½") top and bottom borders.

If using 1½ yards, cut:
• 8 (6"-wide) crosswise strips. Piece as necessary to make 4 borders.

From medium green print, cut:
• 8 (2¼"-wide) strips for straight-grain binding. ➡

Block Assembly

1. Referring to *Rail Fence Cutting Diagram*, join 1 matching light strip to each long side of 1 dark strip. Press seams toward dark strip. Cut strip set into 4 (3½"-wide) Rail Fence units.

2. Referring to *Block Assembly Diagram*, lay out 4 matching Rail Fence units as shown with 1 green center square, 4 green side setting triangles, and 4 green corner setting triangles. Join units in diagonal rows; press seam allowances toward green print. Join rows to complete block (*Block Diagram*).

3. Make 30 blocks.

Quilt Assembly

1. Arrange pieced blocks, setting squares, and setting triangles as shown in *Quilt Top Assembly Diagram*. Join in diagonal rows; press seam allowances toward setting pieces. Join rows to complete quilt top.

2. Add 2 (6" x 72½") side borders. Add 2 (6" x 71½") top and bottom borders.

Quilting and Finishing

1. Divide backing fabric into 2 (2½-yard) lengths. Cut 1 piece in half lengthwise. Sew 1 narrow panel to each side of wide panel. Press seam allowances toward narrow panels.

2. Layer backing, batting, and quilt top; baste. Quilt as desired. Quilt shown is grid-quilted in 3" squares.

3. Join 2¼"-wide medium green strips into 1 continuous strip for French-fold straight-grain binding. Add binding to quilt.

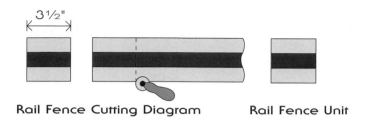

3½"

Rail Fence Cutting Diagram   Rail Fence Unit

Block Assembly Diagram

Block Diagram

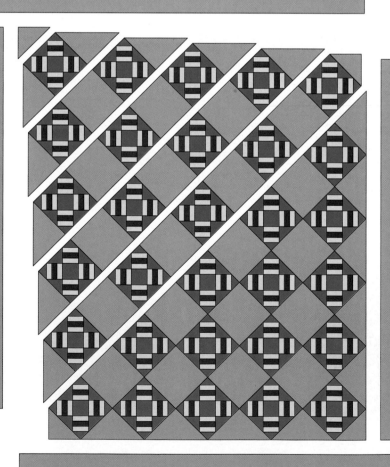

Quilt Top Assembly Diagram

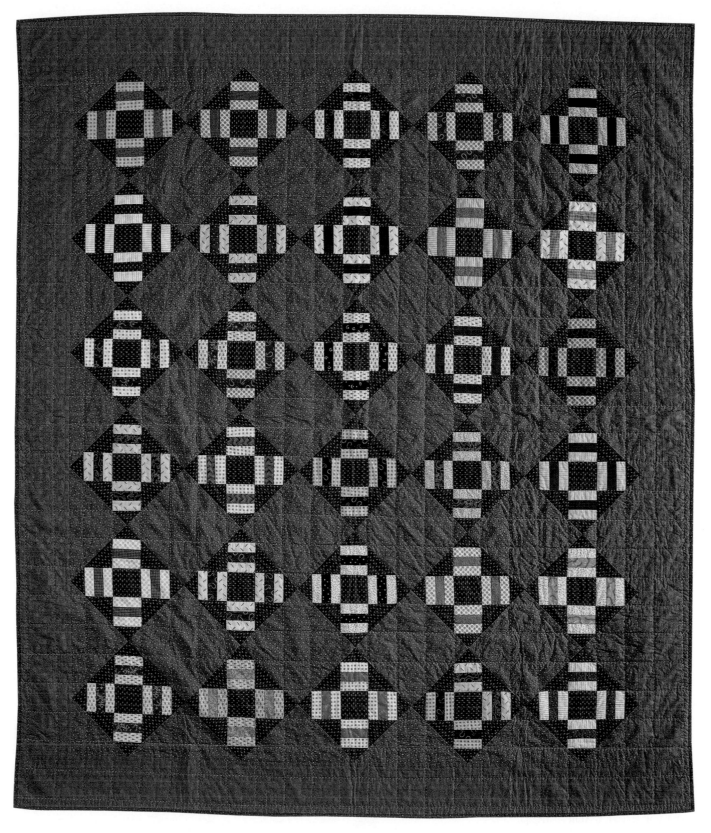

Quilt by Connie Tilman

French Country Strippy Quilt

Marianne Fons and Liz Porter made this quilt for the Roommates Challenge, shown at the 1996 Houston Quilt Festival and Market. The fabrics shown in this quilt were provided by Clothworks division of FASCO, from the Roommates Collection designed by Nancy Martin. Participants had to use some of all the fabrics in the collection and could add a limited number of other fabrics.

Finished Size: 76½" x 99¾"
Blocks: 18 (10") Basket Blocks

Materials

2½ yards tan background lengthwise stripe (Quilt shown uses 10"-wide stripe.)*
2½ yards green background lengthwise stripe (Quilt shown uses 8"-wide stripe.)*
2¼ yards rust paisley print for setting triangles
1⅓ yards tan fabric for block backgrounds
Fat quarter** each of 3 red prints and 3 green prints for baskets (Each fabric is used for 3 baskets.)
Fat eighth*** each of 6 prints (3 prints to coordinate with red fabrics and 3 with green fabrics to make 3 baskets from each fabric)
¾ yard fabric for binding
6 yards fabric for backing
*Note: If your fabric's stripe is not this wide, consider piecing strips to achieve desired width.
**Fat quarter = 18" x 22"
***Fat eighth = 9" x 22"

Cutting

Measurements include ¼" seam allowances. Cut crosswise strips for all fabrics except border stripes. Borders are cut longer than needed. Trim borders to size before sewing to quilt. Side-setting triangles are cut larger than needed and trimmed to size after rows are assembled.

From rust paisley print, cut:
• 8 (15½") squares. Cut squares in quarters diagonally to make 32 side setting triangles. (You will have 2 extra.)
• 6 (8") squares. Cut squares in half diagonally to make 12 corner setting triangles.

From tan background fabric, cut:
• 4 (2⅞"-wide) strips. Cut strips into 54 (2⅞") squares. Cut squares in half diagonally to make 108 A triangles.
• 2 (2½"-wide) strips. Cut strips into 18 (2½") B squares.
• 2 (4⅞"-wide) strips. Cut strips into 9 (4⅞") squares.

Cut squares in half diagonally to make 18 C triangles.
• 6 (2½"-wide) strips. Cut strips into 36 (2½" x 6½") D rectangles.

From each red and green fabric, cut:
• 3 (2⅞" x 22") strips. Cut strips into 18 (2⅞") squares. Cut squares in half diagonally to make 36 A triangles.
• 2 (4⅞") squares. Cut squares in half diagonally to make 4 C triangles. (You will have 1 extra.)

From each coordinating print, cut:
• 3 (2⅞") squares. Cut squares in half diagonally to make 6 A triangles.
• 3 (4⅞") squares. Cut squares in half diagonally to make 6 C triangles.

From fabric with tan background stripe, cut:
• 2 (10" x 89") strips for center sashing.

→

From fabric with green background stripe, cut:

- 4 (8" x 89") strips for outer borders.

Block Assembly

1. Referring to *Block Diagram*, select a red print, coordinating print, and background pieces for 1 block.

2. Referring to *Triangle-square Diagram*, join red A triangles and background print A triangles along long sides to make 6 triangle-squares. Make 2 triangle-squares by combining red A triangles with coordinating print A triangles. Make 1 triangle-square by combining red C triangle with coordinating print C triangle.

3. Referring to *Basket Center Diagram*, add a red A triangle to side of red/coordinating print triangle-square. Join unit to side of C triangle-square. Repeat for adjacent side of C triangle-square. Add a coordinating print C triangle to top edge of basket center unit.

4. Referring to *Basket Assembly Diagram*, join 3 red/background print triangle-squares each into 2 strips. Sew 1 strip to 1 side of center unit. Add a B square to remaining strip and sew to adjacent side of center unit.

5. Join a red A triangle to 1 short end of each D rectangle as shown. Join to lower sides of basket. Sew a background C triangle to bottom corner of block.

6. Repeat to make 9 red baskets and 9 green baskets (*Block Diagram*).

Quilt Assembly

1. Referring to photograph and to *Row Assembly Diagram*, lay out blocks and setting triangles in 3 vertical rows with 6 baskets in each row.

2. Join blocks and setting triangles into rows. Use rotary cutter and long ruler to trim excess fabric along edges of rows to straighten rows as needed. (Remember to leave a ¼" seam allowance beyond corners of blocks as you trim.)

3. Measure length of 1 row. Trim 2 tan sashing strips and 2 green outer borders to this length (approximately 85½"). Lay out block rows, sashing, and borders. Join together. Press seam allowances toward borders and sashing.

4. Measure quilt width. Trim 2 green borders to this length (approximately 77"). Sew green borders to top and bottom edges. Press seam allowances toward borders.

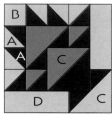

Block Diagram

Triangle-square Diagram

Basket Center Diagram

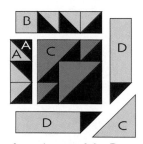

Basket Assembly Diagram

Row Assembly Diagram

Quilting and Finishing

1. Divide backing fabric into 2 (3-yard) pieces. Cut 1 panel in half lengthwise. Stitch a half panel to each long side of full panel.

2. Layer backing, batting, and quilt top. Baste.

3. Quilt as desired. On quilt shown, blocks and setting triangles were quilted in a diagonally set grid of 2" squares by following the lines established by the basket pieces. Borders were quilted by outline quilting around the large flowers.

4. From binding fabric, make approximately 370" of French-fold binding. Add binding to quilt.

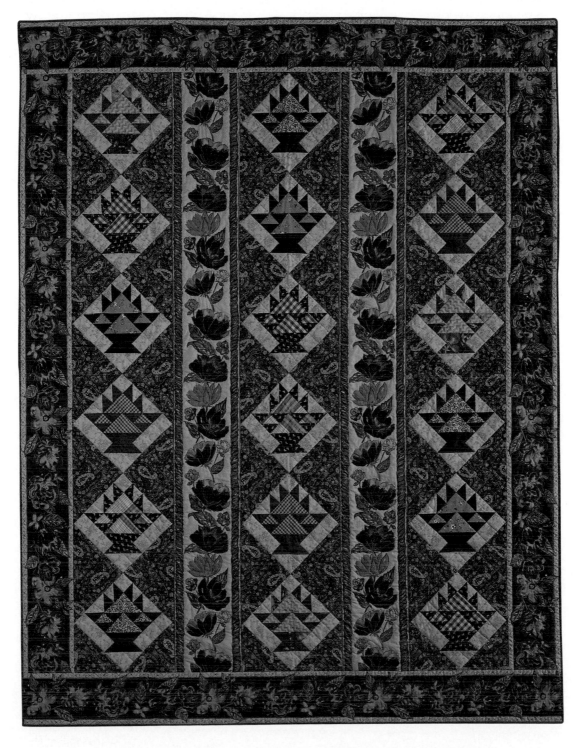

Quilt by Marianne Fons and Liz Porter; machine-quilted by Fern Stewart

Flamingo Fun

If it's just too hot to work on a bed-size quilt, try these fun flamingos!
Add Florida flair to a kitchen, a bathroom, or a teen's room.

Materials

1 fat quarter* each of 3 pink
  fabrics for flamingos
1 fat quarter* each of 3 background fabrics (Quilt shown
  has 2 solid blacks and 1
  dark purple.)
¾ yard tropical print for border
Scrap of white with black dots
  for eyes**
⅜ yard small pink print for
  binding
1½ yards fabric for backing
30" x 48" piece of batting
*Fat quarter = 18" x 22"
**May substitute with buttons
  or plastic jiggle eyes.

Cutting

Measurements include ¼"
seam allowances. Cut crosswise strips unless otherwise
noted. Border strips are exact
length needed. You may want
to cut them longer to allow for
piecing variations.

From each pink fabric, cut:
• 1 (1¼" x 20") strip (A).
• 6 (2") squares (B).
• 1 (3⅞") square. Cut square in
  half diagonally to make 2
  half-square triangles (C).
• 1 (1¼" x 3½") rectangle (D).
• 1 (3½") square (F).

From background fabrics, cut:
• 3 sets of:
  • 1 (1¼" x 20") strip (A).
  • 5 (2") squares (B).
  • 1 (3⅞") square. Cut square
    in half diagonally to make 2
    half-square triangles (C).
  • 1 (2" x 4¼") rectangle (E).
  • 2 (3½") squares (F).
  • 1 (2" x 3½") rectangle (G).

• 1 (5") square (H).
• 1 (3½" x 6½") rectangle (I).
• 1 (6½") square (J).

From tropical print, cut:
• 3 (6"-wide) strips. Cut strips
  into 2 (6" x 15½") side border
  strips and 2 (6" x 43") top
  and bottom border strips.

*If fabric is narrower than 43",
use leftovers from the side
borders to piece longer top and
bottom borders. —Marianne*

From white-with-black-dots
fabric, cut:
• 3 (⅞") circles, centering dot
  in each.

From small pink print, cut:
• 4 (2¼"-wide) strips for
  binding.

Block Assembly

Refer to *Block Assembly
Diagram* throughout.

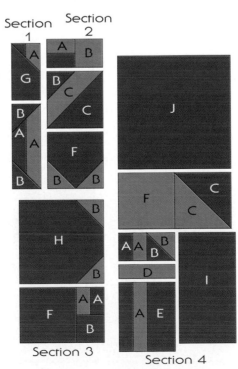

Block Assembly Diagram

1. Join 1 background A strip
to 1 pink A strip along long
sides. Press seam allowance
to dark side. Cut the following
segments from strip set: 1 (5"-
wide) piece, 1 (4¼"-wide)
piece, and 4 (2"-wide) pieces.
2. Using diagonal seams, lay
1 background B square atop
each end of 5"-wide A strip
set. Stitch diagonally, as
shown in *Diagram 1*. Trim and
press open.
3. Lay 1 (2"-wide) A strip set
atop 1 G as shown in *Diagram
2*. Join with a diagonal seam.
Trim and press open. Join with
A/B unit to make Section #1.
4. Join 1 (2"-wide) A strip set
to 1 pink B to make an A/B
unit.
5. Join 1 pink C and 1 background C to make a half-
square triangle unit. Lay 1
background B atop corner of
pink C triangle unit as shown
in *Diagram 3*. Stitch diagonally
as shown, trim, and press
open to make a B/C unit.

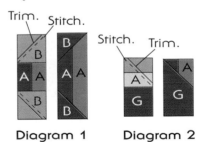

Diagram 1   Diagram 2

Diagram 3

6. Using diagonal seams, join 1 pink B to corner of 1 background F. Repeat for adjacent corner to make 1 B/F unit (*Diagram 4.*) Join units as shown to complete Section #2.

7. Using diagonal seams, join 1 pink B to 1 H as shown in Section #3. Repeat on adjacent corner to make 1 B/H unit. Join 1 (2"-wide) A strip set to 1 background B. Join A/B unit to 1 background F. Join to B/H unit to complete Section #3.

8. Using diagonal seams, join 1 background B and 1 pink B into 1 half-square triangle unit (*Diagram 5*). Trim and press open. Join with 1 (2"-wide) A strip set. Add 1 pink D to bottom of unit. Join 4¼" A strip set to 1 background E. Join to bottom of A/B/D unit. Join 1 background I to right side of A/B/D/E unit. Join 1 background C and 1 pink C to make 1 half-square triangle unit. Join to 1 pink F. Join units and background J as shown to complete Section #4.

9. Join Section #1 and #2. Add Section #3 to bottom. Join to Section #4 to complete block. Appliqué circle in position for eye. Make 3 blocks (*Block Diagram*).

Quilt Assembly

1. Referring to photo, join 3 blocks into a strip.

2. Add 6" x 15½" borders to opposite sides of quilt top. Press seam allowance toward borders. Add 6" x 43" borders to quilt top and bottom.

Quilting and Finishing

1. Layer backing, batting, and quilt top; baste. Quilt as desired. Quilt shown was quilted around and through flamingo bodies with diagonal lines in background. Border is quilted in diagonals.

2. Join 2¼"-wide small pink print strips into 1 continuous piece for straight-grain French-fold binding. Add binding to quilt.

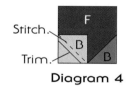

Stitch. Trim.

Diagram 4

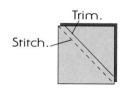

Trim. Stitch.

Diagram 5

Block Diagram

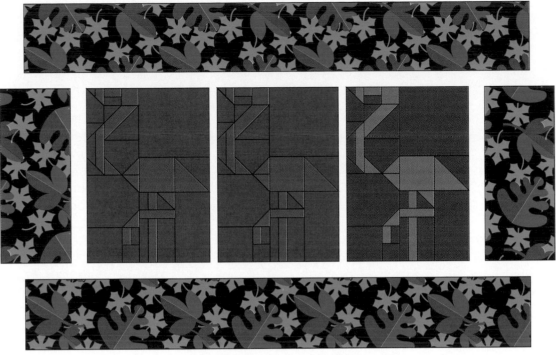

Quilt Top Assembly Diagram

Quilt by Sara Nephew

Album Cross

This block shows up in many quilts from the Civil War era. Quilters would often cut the center square from muslin or a light print, which could be inked with signatures. Striped fabrics were popular for the sashing, borders, and blocks.

Finished Size: 94" x 94"
Blocks: 64 (8") Album
Cross Blocks

Materials
3 yards light yellow solid for background
14 fat quarters* dark prints for blocks (Quilt shown has 6 blues, 5 golds, and 3 browns.)
2½ yards blue print for sashing strips
⅝ yard gold print for sashing squares
1⅞ yards blue/gold/brown print for borders
7½ yards fabric for backing
King-size batting
¾ yard fabric for binding
12" or 12½" square ruler
*Fat quarter = 18" x 22"

Cutting
Measurements include ¼" seam allowances. Cut crosswise strips unless otherwise noted.

From light yellow solid, cut:
• 13 (7½"-wide) strips. Cut strips into 64 (7½") squares. Cut squares into quarters diagonally to make 256 quarter-square triangles for block background (C).

From dark prints, cut:

• 7 (2½" x 22") strips from each. Cut strips into 64 sets of 4 matching 2½" x 5½" pieces for B (256 total) and 64 (2½") squares for A.

From blue print, cut:
• 29 (2½"-wide) strips. Cut each strip into 5 (2½" x 8½") pieces to make 144 sashing strips. (You will have 1 extra.)

From gold print, cut:
• 5 (2½"-wide) strips. Cut each strip into 17 (2½") squares to make 81 sashing squares. (You will have 4 extra.)

From the blue/gold/brown print, cut:
•9 (6½"-wide) strips for borders. Join 4 strips to make 2 (6½" x 82½") borders. Join 5 strips to make 2 (6½" x 94½") borders.

From backing fabric, cut:
• 2 (3-yard) lengths.
• 1 (1½-yard) length. Cut in half lengthwise. Rejoin halves into 1 long strip.

From binding fabric, cut:
• 10 (2¼"-wide) strips.

Block Assembly
1. Referring to *Block Assembly Diagram*, arrange pieces for 1 block as shown. Join 1 A between 2 Bs. Join 1 C to each side of remaining 2 Bs. *Note: The triangles are oversized and cross rectangles are longer than needed. You will trim them to size later.*
2. From typing paper, cut a 2" square. Referring to *Cutting Guide*, align 2 adjacent corners of paper square with 4¼" marks on square ruler. Tape square to ruler.
3. Place prepared rotary-cutting square over block, aligning paper square over ➡

Block Assembly Diagram

Block Diagram

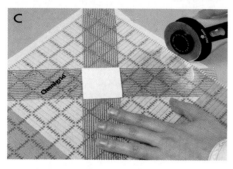

block center. Trim 2 sides (photos A and B). Turn block and reposition ruler so that trimmed edges align with 8½" marks, and then trim remaining 2 sides (photo C). This method ensures that your center square is centered and that block measures 8½" (photo D).
4. Repeat to make 64 blocks, as shown in *Block Diagram*.

Quilt Assembly

1. Referring to *Sashing Row Assembly Diagram*, join 9 sashing strips and 8 blocks as shown. Press seam allowances toward sashing strips. Make 8 block rows.
2. Referring to *Block Row Assembly Diagram*, join 9 sashing strips and 8 blocks as shown. Press seam allowances toward sashing

strips. Make 8 block rows.
3. Referring to photo, join sashing rows and block rows alternately to make quilt top.
4. Join 6½" x 82½" borders to quilt sides. Join 6½" x 94½" borders to quilt top and bottom.

Quilting and Finishing

1. To make backing, join 2 wide outer panels and 1 narrow middle panel. Press seams away from middle panel.
2. Layer backing, batting, and quilt top. Baste. Quilt as desired. Quilt shown was machine-quilted with a leaf wreath over blocks and meandering leaf pattern in borders.
3. Join 2¼"-wide binding strips into 1 continuous piece for French-fold straight-grain binding. Add binding to quilt.

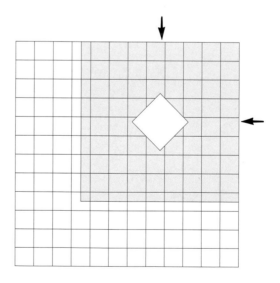

Cutting Guide

Sashing Row Assembly Diagram

Block Row Assembly Diagram

Quilt by Rhonda Richards; machine-quilted by New Traditions

Crow's Feet

Members of the Rather Bees quilting bee of Des Moines made Crow's Feet blocks to celebrate the 50th birthday of member Mary B. Larson. They had set them together at a party in her honor. Later that day, Mary B. became ill at home. Her heart, damaged by several attacks, was not strong enough to recover. Mary B., beloved by many, did not regain consciousness. The Rather Bees finished the quilt and gave it to her husband David and son Sean.

Finished Size: $74\frac{1}{2}$" x $76\frac{1}{2}$"
Blocks: 36 ($6\frac{7}{8}$") Crow's Feet Blocks

Materials
36 assorted fat eighths* light prints for blocks
36 assorted fat eighths* dark prints for blocks
4 yards brown print for setting pieces and pieced borders (5 yards for unpieced borders)
$1\frac{1}{4}$ yards black for pieced border and binding (2 yards for unpieced borders)
$4\frac{3}{4}$ yards fabric for backing
Full-size batting
*Fat eighth = 9" x 22"

Cutting
Measurements include $\frac{1}{4}$" seam allowances. Blocks are set on point in columns, and there is $\frac{1}{4}$" between each block and side or border seam line. This makes blocks "float"

against Streak of Lightning setting fabric.

From each light print, cut:
• 9 ($1\frac{7}{8}$") squares (C).
• 2 ($2\frac{5}{8}$") squares. Cut squares in quarters diagonally to make 8 quarter-square triangles (A).

From each dark print, cut:
• 2 ($1\frac{7}{8}$" x $4\frac{5}{8}$") rectangles (D).
• 2 ($1\frac{7}{8}$") squares (C).
• 4 ($2\frac{1}{4}$") squares. Cut squares in half diagonally to make 8 half-square triangles (B).
• 2 ($2\frac{5}{8}$") squares. Cut squares in quarters diagonally to make 8 quarter-square triangles (A).

From brown print, cut:
• 8 (6"-wide) strips. Piece strips to make 2 (6" x 80") top and bottom borders and 2 (6" x 83") side borders. For unpieced borders, cut 4 (6" x 90") lengthwise strips. Trim after adding to quilt and

mitering corners.
• 1 ($11\frac{1}{8}$"-wide) strip. Cut strip into 3 ($11\frac{1}{8}$") squares. Cut squares in half diagonally to make 6 half-square setting triangles (X).
• 1 (6"-wide) strip. Cut strip into 6 (6") squares. Cut squares in half diagonally to make 12 half-square setting triangles (Y).
• 6 ($11\frac{1}{2}$"-wide) strip. Cut strip into 17 ($11\frac{1}{2}$") squares. Cut squares in quarters diagonally to make 66 quarter-square setting triangles (Z). (You will have 2 extra.)

From black, cut:
• 8 ($1\frac{1}{2}$"-wide) strips. Piece to make 4 ($1\frac{1}{2}$" x 72") borders. For unpieced borders, cut 4 ($1\frac{1}{2}$" x 72") lengthwise strips. Trim after adding to quilt and mitering corners.
• 8 ($2\frac{1}{4}$"-wide) strips for binding (10 strips if using unpieced border leftovers). ➤

Block Assembly

1. Join 1 dark A to 1 light A to make a triangle. Join to a matching dark B triangle to make a square point unit. Make 4 left and 4 right point units as shown in *Point Unit Diagrams*.

2. Lay out 9 light Cs, 2 dark cs, 2 dark Ds, and 8 point units as shown in *Block Assembly Diagram*. Join into rows; join rows to complete block (*Block Diagram*).

3. Make 36 blocks. For variety, you can make point units from 1 fabric and dark Cs and Ds from another.

Quilt Assembly

1. Referring to *Quilt Top Assembly Diagram*, arrange blocks in 6 columns of 6 blocks as shown.

2. Join 2 Z setting triangles to each side of 30 blocks as shown. Note: Setting pieces are slightly larger to allow blocks to "float" between columns. Join 1 Z and 1 Y triangle to sides of 6 blocks as shown. Join blocks in each column in diagonal rows, matching block points. Add X and Y setting triangles to ends of columns.

3. Using long ruler and rotary cutter, trim sides of rows ½" beyond corners of blocks.

4. Join columns.

5. Center and sew black borders to each brown border. Press seam allowance toward brown borders. Center and sew borders to quilt sides; miter border corners.

Quilting and Finishing

1. Divide backing fabric into 2 (2⅜-yard) lengths. Cut 1 piece in half lengthwise. Join 1 narrow panel to each side of wide panel. Press seam allowances toward narrow panels.

2. Layer backing, batting, and quilt top; baste. Quilt as desired. Quilt shown was quilted in-the-ditch around dark portion of each block and outline-quilted ¼" inside each block. Setting triangles and borders have feather pattern.

3. Join 2¼"-wide black strips into 1 continuous piece for French-fold straight-grain binding. Add binding to quilt.

Left Point Unit Diagram   **Right Point Unit Diagram**

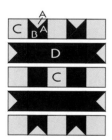

Block Assembly Diagram

Block Diagram

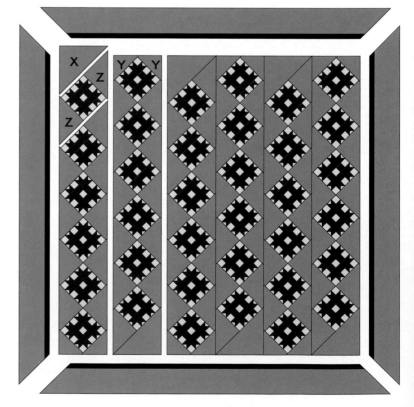

Quilt Top Assembly Diagram

Quilt by the Rather Bees

Mad for Plaid

Lyn Mann is mad about plaids. In fact, she makes a new plaid quilt each year and then teaches a quilt class based on it to justify her ever-growing collection! If plaids are your passion, what better way to showcase them than in this scrappy quilt?

Finished Size: 64" x 88"
Blocks: 38 (6") Ivy Blocks

Materials

1¼ yards total assorted dark plaids for blocks
⅝ yard total assorted medium plaids for blocks
18 fat quarters* assorted light prints and plaids for blocks and sashing
10 fat quarters* assorted blue plaids and stripes for sashing, inner border, and sawtooth border
2¼ yards cream and tan prints for borders
¾ yard blue plaid for binding
5½ yards fabric for backing
Twin-size batting
*Fat quarter = 18" x 22"

Cutting

Measurements include ¼" seam allowances.

From dark plaids, cut:
• 38 sets (for blocks) of:
  • 5 (1⅞") squares. Cut squares in half diagonally to make 10 A triangles. You will have 1 extra.
  • 1 (3½") E square.
  • 1 (2½") G square.
• 12 sets (for A/B side triangle units) of:

• 3 (1⅞") squares. Cut in half diagonally to make 6 A triangles. You will have 1 extra.

From medium plaids, cut:
• 38 sets (in colors compatible with dark plaid sets for blocks) of:
  • 1 (2½") square B.
  • 1 (2⅞") square. Cut square in half diagonally to make 2 C triangles.
• 12 sets (in colors compatible with dark plaid sets for A/B side triangle units) of:
  • 1 (2½") square B.

From light prints and plaids, cut:
• 38 sets (for blocks) of:
  • 6 (1⅞") squares. Cut squares in half diagonally to make 12 A triangles. You will have 1 extra.
  • 1 (3⅞") square. Cut in half diagonally to make 2 D triangles.
  • 2 (3⅛") F squares.
• 12 sets (for side triangles) of:
  • 3 (1⅞") squares. Cut in half diagonally to make 6 A triangles. You will have 1 extra.
  • 6 (5½") squares. Cut squares in quarters diagonally to make 24 N triangles for side triangles.
  • 144 (2½" x 4½") H rectangles

for Goose Chase sashing units.
• 17 (4½") J squares for sashing squares.
• 2 (9¾") squares. Cut squares in quarters diagonally to make 8 corner triangles. Join in sets of 2 as shown in *Quilt Top Assembly Diagram*.

From blue plaids, cut:
• 356 (2½") squares (I) consisting of 17 sets of 4 (sashing squares) and 144 sets of 2 (Goose Chase sashing units).
• 24–30 (2"-wide x 3"–7"-long) rectangles. Piece to make 2 (2" x 68½") side borders.
• 24–30 (2¾"-wide x 3"–7"-long) rectangles. Piece to make 2 (2¾" x 48½") top and bottom borders.
• 10 (2⅞"-wide) strips. Cut strips into 136 (2⅞") squares. Cut squares in half diagonally to make 272 M half-square triangles for sawtooth border.

From cream print, cut:
• 4 (4½"-wide) lengthwise strips for border. Strips will be approximately 81" long.
• From remainder, cut 17 (2⅞"-wide) crosswise strips. Strips will be approximately 24" long. Cut strips into 136 (2⅞") squares. Cut squares ▶

in half diagonally to make 272 M half-square triangles for sawtooth border.

From blue plaid, cut:
• 8 (2¼"-wide) strips for binding.

Block Assembly

Refer to diagrams throughout.
1. *A/B Unit Assembly*—Join 1 dark A and 1 light A to make a triangle-square. Make 9 A squares. Join 5 A squares and 1 medium B square as shown to make 1 A/B unit.
2. *A/C/D Unit Assembly*—Using remaining A squares, join 2 squares into a strip. Add 1 light A triangle.
3. Join A strip to 1 side of 1 medium C triangle. Add to 1 light D triangle to complete 1 A/C/D Unit for right side of block.
4. Repeat Steps 2 and 3 to make 1 reversed A/C/D unit as shown for left side of block.
5. *E/F/G Unit Assembly*—Using diagonal seams, lay 1 light F atop 1 dark E as shown. Stitch diagonally and trim excess. Repeat on opposite side. Using diagonal seams, join 1 G to corner as shown to complete.
6. Join units as shown in *Ivy Block Assembly Diagram* to make 1 block.
7. Make 38 Ivy Blocks. Join 4 blocks as shown in *Four-Block Unit Diagram*. Make 8 Four-Block Units.
8. Referring to Step 1, make 60 A squares; then make 12 A/B units. Join 2 light N triangles to each as shown in *Side Triangle Diagram*. Join these pieced triangles to each side of remaining 6 Ivy Blocks to make 6 Side Triangle Units.

A/B Unit Assembly

A/C/D Unit Assembly

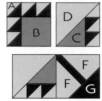
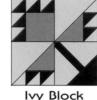

E/F/G Unit Assembly

Ivy Block Assembly Diagram   **Ivy Block Diagram**

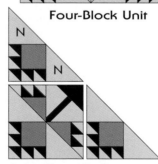

Four-Block Unit

Side Triangle Diagram

Sashing Unit Assembly

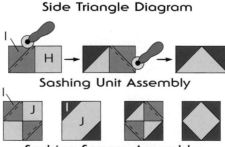

Sashing Square Assembly

Sawtooth Border Assembly

Sashing Assembly

Refer to diagrams throughout.
1. *Sashing Unit Assembly*—Using diagonal seams, join 2 matching dark Is to ends of 1 light H. Trim and press open. Make 144 Goose Chase units. Join into 24 (6-unit) strips.
2. *Sashing Square Assembly*—Using diagonal seams, join 4 matching dark Is to corners of 1 light J to make 1 sashing square. Trim and press open. Make 17 sashing squares.
3. *Sawtooth Border Assembly*—Join 1 dark M and 1 light M as shown. Make 272 M triangle-squares. Join M squares into 2 (36-unit), 2 (26-unit), 2 (42-unit), and 2 (32-unit) half-square triangle borders. Refer to photo on page 100 for orientation.

Quilt Assembly

1. Lay out all units as shown in *Quilt Top Assembly Diagram*. Join into rows. Join rows to complete center. Trim sashing squares even with quilt top.
2. Add blue 2"-wide side borders to opposite sides of quilt top. Press seam allowance toward borders. Measure width of quilt, including borders. If necessary, trim side borders evenly so quilt is 48½" wide. This will ensure that sawtooth borders will fit. Join blue 2¾"-wide borders to top and bottom of quilt. Measure length of quilt and trim blue borders evenly if necessary so quilt measures 72½" long.
3. Add 1 (36-unit) sawtooth border to each side of quilt. Add 1 (26-unit) sawtooth border to top and bottom.

4. Trim 2 cream borders to 76½" long. Add to quilt sides. Trim remaining 2 cream borders to 60½" long. Add to quilt top and bottom.
5. Add 42-unit half-square triangle borders to quilt sides and 32-unit half-square triangle borders to quilt top and bottom.

Quilting and Finishing

1. Divide backing fabric into 2 (2¾-yard) lengths. Cut 1 piece in half lengthwise. Sew 1 narrow panel to each side of wide panel. Press seam allowance toward narrow panels.
2. Layer backing, batting, and quilt top; baste. Quilt as desired. Quilt shown was outline-quilted around all patchwork. Cream border has a feather pattern, and background is filled with stipple quilting. Light areas of blocks are also stippled.
3. Join 2¼"-wide blue plaid strips into 1 continuous piece for straight-grain French-fold binding. Add binding to quilt.

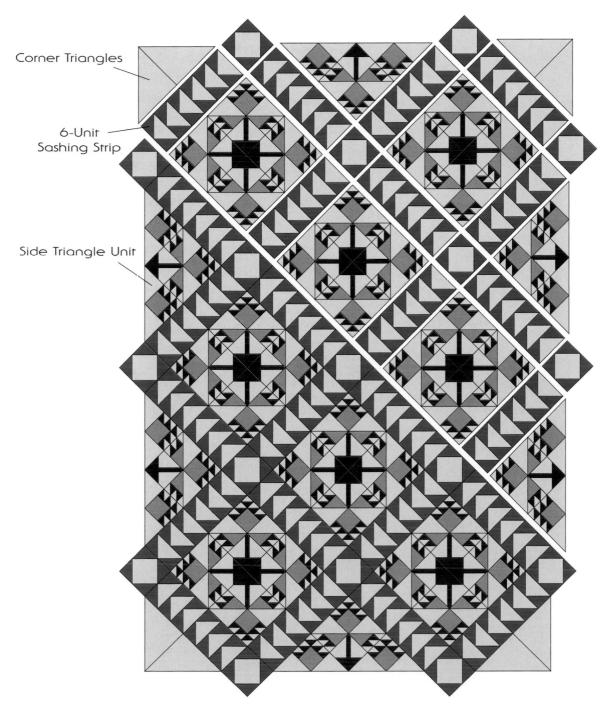

Corner Triangles

6-Unit Sashing Strip

Side Triangle Unit

Quilt Top Assembly Diagram

Quilt by Lynn Oser Mann

Scrappy Star

If you collect fabric squares or have thought about exchanging squares with your friends, this is the quilt for you! The design also works well for fat quarters. Using a solid fabric and diagonal seams, you'll be seeing stars in no time. ➞

Finished Size: 71" x 89"

Materials

16 fat quarters* of assorted prints and plaids
2¾ yards solid white for stars
1¼ yards solid green for inner border and binding
1¼ yards green plaid for outer pieced border (2½ yards for unpieced border)
5½ yards fabric for backing
Twin-size batting
*Fat quarter = 18" x 22"

Cutting

Measurements include ¼" seam allowances. Border strips are exact length needed. You may want to cut them longer to allow for piecing variations.

From each fat quarter, cut:
• 4 (4½" x 22") strips. Cut strips into:
  • 9 (4½") squares (D). You will have 14 extra Ds.
  • 18 (2½" x 4½") rectangles (B). You will have 5 extra Bs.

*I*f you collect 4½" fabric squares, you'll need:
• 130 (4½") squares (D).
• 283 (2½" x 4½") rectangles (B).
—Liz

From solid white, cut:
• 10 (2½"-wide) strips. Cut strips into 154 (2½") squares (C).
• 44 (1½"-wide) strips. Cut strips into 1,232 (1½") squares (A).

From solid green, cut:
• 9 (1½"-wide) strips. Cut strips into 46 (1½" x 4½") rectangles (F), 50 (1½" x 2½") rectangles (E) and 4 (1½") squares (G).

• 8 (2¼"-wide) strips for binding.

From green plaid, cut:
• 8 (4"-wide) strips for border. Piece to make 2 (4" x 82½") side borders and 2 (4" x 71½") top and bottom borders. If you prefer unpieced borders, cut 4 (4"-wide) lengthwise strips from alternate yardage and trim to above lengths.

Unit Assembly

1. Referring to *Diagonal Seams Diagrams*, place 1 A atop 1 end of 1 green E. Stitch diagonally as shown and trim ¼" from stitching. Press open. Repeat for opposite end to make 1 border point unit. Make 50 border point units.
2. Using diagonal seams as above, join 1 A to 1 corner of 1 B. Trim and press open. Repeat for all 4 corners. Make 283 sashing point units.

Trim.

Stitch. **Diagonal Seams Diagrams**

Sashing Point Unit

Row Assembly

1. Join 11 border point units, 10 Fs, and 2 Gs as shown in *Border Row Diagram*. Make 2 Border Rows.
2. Join 2 border point units, 10 sashing point units, and 11 white C squares as shown in *Row 1 Diagram*. Make 14 of Row 1.
3. Join 2 Fs, 11 sashing point units, and 10 print D squares as shown in *Row 2 Diagram*. Make 13 of Row 2.

Quilt Assembly

1. Lay out Rows 1 and 2, alternating rows. Join rows, matching seams. Add 1 border row each to top and bottom of quilt, matching seams.
2. Add plaid side borders to opposite sides of quilt top. Press seam allowance toward borders. Join remaining plaid borders to top and bottom of quilt.

Border Point Unit

G   F

Border Row

Row 1

F

Row 2

Row Assembly Diagrams

Quilting and Finishing

1. Divide backing fabric into 2 (2¾-yard) lengths. Cut 1 piece in half lengthwise. Sew 1 narrow panel to each side of wide panel. Press seam allowances toward narrow panels.

2. Layer backing, batting, and quilt top; baste. Quilt as desired. Quilt shown was quilted diagonally through each C and D square and in a grid through center of each C square and sashing point unit.

Borders are meander-quilted.

3. Join 2¼"-wide solid green strips into 1 continuous piece for straight-grain French-fold binding. Add binding to quilt.

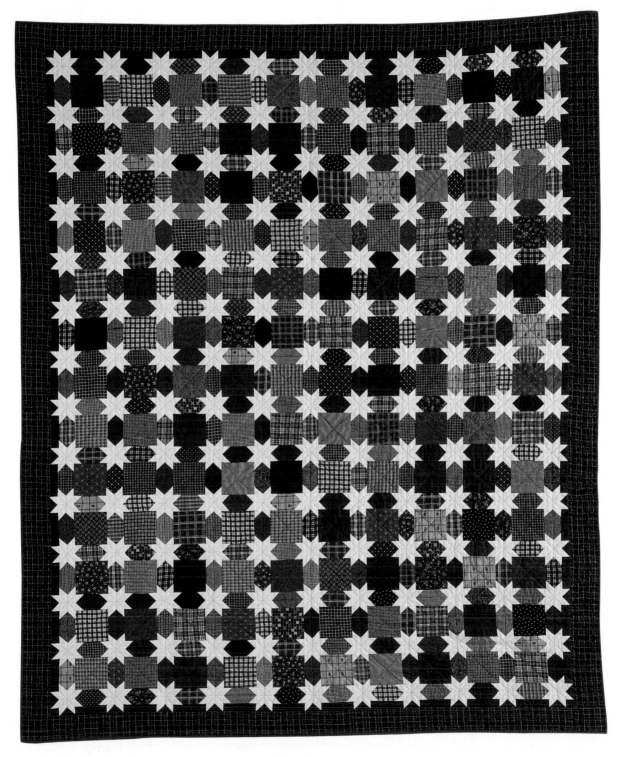

Quilt by Rayetta M. Bate

Double X

Quiltmaker Connie Tilman has a knack for making new quilts that look like antiques. One of her tricks is to mix and match the same or similar dark fabrics within some blocks to make it look like she ran out of fabric and was "making do" with scraps.

Finished Size: 75" x 87¾"
Blocks: 20 (9") Double X
Blocks

Materials
10 fat quarters* assorted dark prints (black, gold, red, pink, blue) for blocks and pieced border
10 fat quarters* assorted shirting prints for blocks and pieced border
1 yard black print for inner border
¾ yard black stripe for binding
5–8 fat quarters* assorted black prints for setting triangles
1 yard medium pink print for setting blocks
1½ yards dark pink print for outer border
5½ yards fabric for backing
Full-size batting
*Fat quarter = 18" x 22"

Cutting
Measurements include ¼" seam allowances. Cut crosswise strips unless otherwise noted. Mix and match prints as desired.

From each dark fat quarter, cut:
• 4 (3⅞") squares. Cut squares in half diagonally to make 8 E half-square triangles.
• 2 (3½") C squares.

• 12 (2⅜") squares. Cut squares in half diagonally to make 24 A half-square triangles.
• 6 (3½") squares for pieced border.

From each shirting fat quarter, cut:
• 4 (3") squares. Cut squares in half diagonally to make 8 D half-square triangles.
• 12 (2⅜") squares. Cut squares in half diagonally to make 24 A half-square triangles.
• 8 (2" x 3½") B rectangles.
• 3 (3½") squares for pieced border.

From black border print, cut:
• 7 (3½"-wide) strips. Piece to make 2 (3½" x 70") side border strips and 2 (3½" x 65") top and bottom border strips.

From black stripe, cut:
• 9 (2¼"-wide) strips for binding.

From assorted black fat quarters, cut:
• 4 (15") squares. Cut squares in quarters diagonally to make 14 quarter-square side setting triangles. You will have 2 extra. You may cut as many or as few repeats as you wish. The triangles are

oversize, and the quilt as shown has ½" between block corner and border.
• 2 (8½") squares. Cut squares in half diagonally to make 4 corner half-square setting triangles. You may cut these from 4 different prints if you prefer. Triangles are oversize. Quilt shown has ½" between block corners and border.
• 2 (3½") squares for pieced border.

From medium pink print, cut:
• 3 (9½"-wide) strips. Cut strips into 12 (9½") setting squares.

From dark pink print, cut:
• 8 (6"-wide) strips. Piece to make 2 (6" x 80") side borders and 2 (6" x 76") top and bottom borders.

Block Assembly

Quiltmaker Connie Tilman cut matching sets of dark and light pieces for her 20 blocks, but mixed a few of them when she made the blocks to give her quilt a more old-fashioned look. —Marianne

1. Join 1 light A and 1 dark A into a triangle-square. Make 12 A units. ➡

2. Join 1 light D to each side of 1 dark C. Join 1 dark E to each side of C/D unit as shown in *C/D/E Unit Assembly Diagram*.

3. Lay out C/D/E unit with 12 A units and 4 light B rectangles as shown in *Block Assembly Diagram*. Join into sections; join sections to complete block.

4. Make 20 blocks as shown in *Block Diagram*, mixing prints as desired.

C/D/E Unit Assembly Diagram

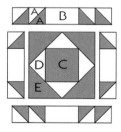

Block Assembly Diagram

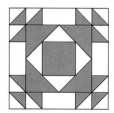

Block Diagram

Quilt Assembly

1. Lay out blocks, setting squares, and setting triangles as shown in *Quilt Top Assembly Diagram*. Join into diagonal rows; join rows to complete quilt.

2. Use 24"-long ruler and rotary cutter to trim all sides of quilt ¾" from corners of blocks, so that black border will float ½" from blocks.

3. Measure length of quilt. Trim black side borders to size and add to opposite sides of quilt top. Press seam allowance toward borders. Measure width of quilt, including borders. Trim remaining 2 black borders to size. Join to top and bottom of quilt.

4. Join 24 (3½") squares into a strip. Make 2 strips. Add to sides of quilt. Trim to fit, if necessary. Join 21 (3½")

squares into a strip. Make 2 strips. Add to top and bottom of quilt. Trim to fit, if necessary.

5. Measure, trim, and add outer dark pink border to quilt.

Quilting and Finishing

1. Divide backing fabric into 2 (2¾-yard) lengths. Cut 1 piece in half lengthwise. Sew 1 narrow panel to each side of wide panel. Press seam allowance toward narrow panels.

2. Layer backing, batting, and quilt top; baste. Quilt as desired. Quilt shown was utility-quilted with black pearl cotton in a grid pattern. Black border and pieced border are quilted in-the-ditch, with pieced grid extending into outer border.

3. Join 2¼"-wide black stripe strips into 1 continuous piece for straight-grain French-fold binding. Add binding to quilt.

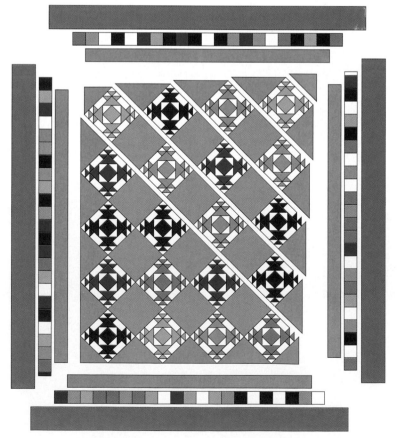

Quilt Top Assembly Diagram

Quilt by Connie Tilman

Mini Mariner's Compass

Making a Mariner's Compass couldn't be easier than with foundation piecing. You'll be surprised how quickly this block comes together! Liz Porter stitched this miniature using fabrics from Fons & Porter's Cumberland Collection by Benartex.

Finished Size: 31½" x 31½"
Blocks: 5 (7") Mariner's Compass Blocks

Materials

Fat eighth* each 5 dark prints for blocks (gold, blue, brown, green, red)
Fat eighth* each 5 medium prints for blocks (gold, blue, brown, green, red)
½ yard light print for background
½ yard green print for sashing and inner border
½ yard cream-and-red print for setting triangles
1⅞ yards large red print for outer border, binding, and backing
38" x 38" batting
*Fat eighth = 9" x 22"

Cutting

Measurements include ¼" seam allowances. Border strips are exact length needed. You may want to cut them longer to allow for piecing variations.

From each dark print, cut:
- 8 (1" x 2½") pieces for compass points #2 and #8.
- 4 (1¼" x 2½") pieces for compass point #5.

- 4 (1¼" x 4") pieces for compass point #12.

From each medium print, cut:
- 8 (1" x 2½") pieces for compass points #1 and #7.
- 4 (1¼" x 2½") pieces for compass point #11.
- 4 (1¼" x 4") pieces for compass point #6.

From light print, cut:
- 4 (2"-wide) strips. Cut strips into 80 (2") squares for background pieces #3, #4, #9, and #10.
- 1 (7½"-wide) strip. Cut strip into 5 (7½") squares for compass backgrounds.

From remaining gold print, cut:
- 12 (1½") squares for sashing squares.

From green print, cut:
- 6 (1½"-wide) strips. Cut strips into:
  - 2 (1½" x 23⅛") strips for top and bottom borders.
  - 2 (1½" x 25⅛") strips for side borders.
  - 16 (1½" x 7½") strips for sashing.

From cream-and-red print, cut:
- 1 (11¼") square. Cut square in quarters diagonally to

make 4 quarter-square side setting triangles.
- 2 (5⅞") squares. Cut squares in half diagonally to make 4 half-square corner setting triangles.

From large red print, cut:
- 1 (33") square for backing.
- 4 (4"-wide) strips. Cut strips into 2 (4" x 25⅛") strips for top and bottom borders and 2 (4" x 32⅛") strips for side borders.
- 4 (2¼"-wide) strips for binding.

Block Assembly

1. Trace or photocopy foundation piecing patterns on page 111. You will need 4 Pattern As and 4 Pattern Bs for each block.

I found it very helpful to have the foundation patterns shaded. It helped me get the fabrics consistently in the same position. —Liz

2. Working with Foundation A, place wrong side of fabric for compass point #1 against unprinted side of area #1 on foundation. Place fabric for compass point #2 right sides facing with first fabric piece. ➤

Align raw edges of fabric pieces so they extend ¼" beyond stitching line that joins #1 and #2. Working from printed side of paper, use a short machine stitch and sew along line between #1 and #2 (photos A and B). Open out dark fabric so it covers area under point #2 and finger-press seam (photo C).

3. Place light print fabric for area #3 right sides facing atop second piece so seam allowance will extend ¼" beyond next stitching line. Stitch along line between #2 and #3 (photos D and E) and trim seam allowance. Open out piece and finger-press (photo F).

4. Continue in this manner (photos G-K) adding pieces in numerical order, until all areas on foundation are covered. Right side of fabric design will be formed on unprinted side of paper foundation. Trim excess fabric and paper along outer dashed line of paper foundation.

5. Stitch 4 Pattern As and 4 Pattern Bs. Join units as shown in *Block Assembly Diagram* and photos L and M to make a circle. Remove paper from wrong side of circle. Baste under ¼" seam allowance around perimeter of circle. Appliqué circle to center of background square. Trim excess fabric from behind compass, leaving ¼" for seam allowance.

6. Make 5 Mariner's Compass blocks, 1 each gold, blue, brown, green, and red.

Quilt Assembly

1. Lay out blocks, sashing, squares, and setting triangles as shown in *Quilt Top Assembly Diagram*. Join into diagonal rows; join rows to complete center. Trim sashing squares along sides even with setting triangles.

2. Add green top and bottom borders; then add green side borders.

3. Repeat to add red borders.

Quilting and Finishing

1. Layer backing, batting, and quilt top; baste. Quilt as desired. Quilt shown was machine-quilted in-the-ditch around compass points and through each point, extending to edge of block. Green borders and sashing are quilted in-the-ditch and have a wave pattern through center. Setting triangles have a feather pattern, and red border is quilted along fabric pattern.

2. Join 2¼"-wide red strips into 1 continuous piece for straight-grain French-fold binding. Add binding to quilt.

A

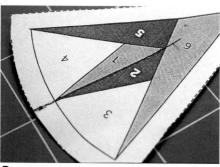

B

C

Block Assembly Diagram

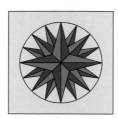

Block Diagram

Quilt Top Assembly Diagram

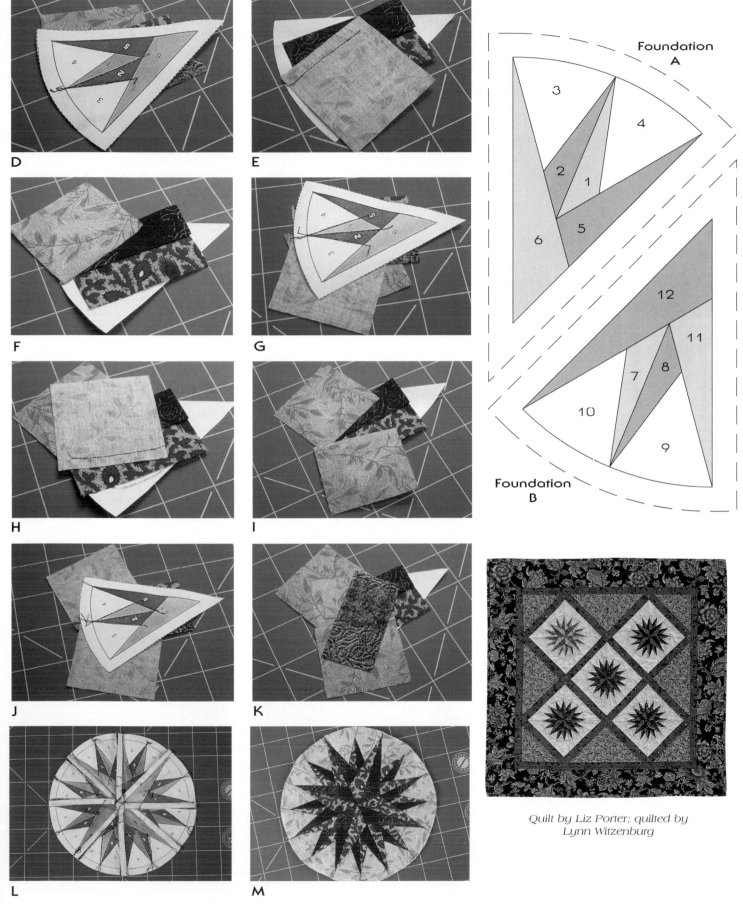

D

E

F

G

H

I

J

K

L

M

Foundation
A

3

4

2

1

5

6

12

11

8

7

10

9

Foundation
B

*Quilt by Liz Porter; quilted by
Lynn Witzenburg*

Collective Conditioning

Dubbed Oklahoma Boomer, this traditional quilt block was first published in 1898 by the Ladies Art Company. Rebecca Rohrkaste used modern fabrics to update the pattern. "The fabrics allowed me some social commentary about urban crowding, social conformity, and environmental conditions," she says.

Finished Size: 75" x 99"
Blocks: 30 (9" x 11")
Oklahoma Boomer Blocks

Materials
30 fat eighths* assorted medium and dark prints for people

30 fat eighths* assorted light prints for block backgrounds

½ yard map print for sashing squares

2¼ yards total assorted prints for sashing

¾ yard brown-and-black print for pieced inner border (2½ yards for unpieced borders)

1 yard total assorted medium prints for triangle border

1 yard total assorted dark prints for triangle border

¼ yard dark blue mottled print for border corners

¾ yard black-and-gold bubble print for binding

6 yards fabric for backing

Queen-size batting

Template material

*Fat eighth = 9" x 22"

Cutting
Measurements include ¼" seam allowances. Cut crosswise strips unless otherwise noted. Border strips are exact length needed. Make templates using patterns on page 115.

From each print for people, cut:
- 1 B, using template.
- 1 (1½" x 1¾") C.
- 2 (1½" x 5½") Ds.
- 1 (3½") square E.
- 2 (1½" x 3½") Gs.

From each light print, cut:
- 1 A, using template.
- 1 A rev., using template.
- 2 (1½" x 1¾") Cs.
- 1 (1½" x 5½") D.

- 2 (3½") squares E.
- 2 (3½" x 7½") Fs.

From map print, cut:
- 4 (3½"-wide) strips. Cut strips into 42 (3½") squares for sashing squares.

From sashing prints, cut:
- 21 (3½"-wide) strips. Cut strips into 35 (3½" x 9½") sashing strips and 36 (3½" x 11½") sashing strips.

From brown-and-black print, cut:
- 9 (2"-wide) strips. Piece to make 2 (2" x 87½") side borders and 2 (2" x 66½") top and bottom borders. If you prefer unpieced borders, cut 4 (2"-wide) lengthwise strips from alternate yardage and proceed.

From medium prints, cut:
- 104 border triangles, using template.

From assorted dark prints, cut:
- 108 border triangles, using template.

From dark blue mottled print, cut:
- 4 border corner pieces, using template.

From black-and-gold bubble print, cut:
- 9 (2¼"-wide) strips for binding.

Block Assembly
1. Referring to *Hat Unit Assembly Diagram*, join 1 A and 1 A rev. to each side of 1 B.

2. Referring to *Head Unit Diagram*, join 1 light C to each side of 1 dark C. Add to A/B unit.

3. Referring to *Leg Unit Diagram*, join 1 dark D to each side of 1 light D.

4. Referring to *Block Assembly Diagram*, join head unit, 1 dark E, and leg unit as shown to make center unit. Join 1 light E and 1 F to each side of 1 G. Repeat. Join to each side of center unit to complete block (*Block Diagram*).

5. Make 30 blocks. ➡

Hat Unit Assembly Diagram

Head Unit Diagram

Leg Unit Diagram

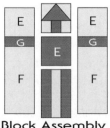

Block Assembly Diagram

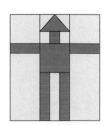

Block Diagram

Border Assembly

1. Referring to *Border Assembly Diagram*, join 1 dark triangle and 1 medium triangle as shown. Continue adding triangles to make outer border triangle strips. Make 2 (23 dark/22 medium) top and bottom border triangle strips and 2 (31 dark/30 medium) side border triangle strips.

2. Add border corner pieces to each end of short border strips.

Border Assembly Diagram

Quilt Assembly

1. Alternate 5 (9½"-long) sashing strips and 6 sashing squares as shown in *Sashing Row Assembly Diagram*. Join into a horizontal row. Make 7 sashing rows.

2. Alternate 5 blocks and 6 (11½"-long) sashing strips as shown in *Block Row Assembly Diagram*. Join into a horizontal row. Make 6 block rows.

3. Alternate sashing rows and block rows as shown in photo. Join rows.

4. Add brown-and-black borders to sides of quilt. Press seam allowance toward borders. Add borders to quilt top and bottom.

5. Add side border triangle strips to quilt, dark triangles to outside. Add top and bottom border triangle strips to quilt. Set in border corner seams.

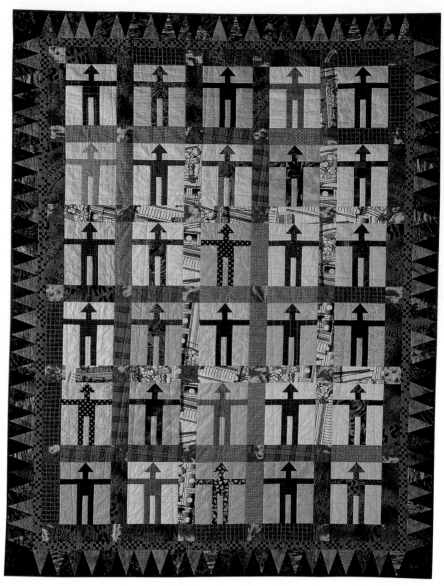

Quilt by Rebecca Rohrkaste

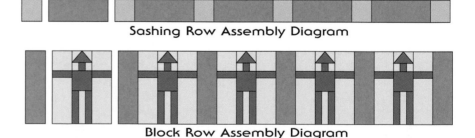

Sashing Row Assembly Diagram

Block Row Assembly Diagram

Quilting and Finishing

1. Divide backing fabric into 2 (3-yard) lengths. Cut 1 piece in half lengthwise. Sew 1 narrow panel to each side of wide panel. Press seam allowances toward narrow panels.

2. Layer backing, batting, and quilt top; baste. Quilt as desired. Quilt shown was quilted in a random grid.

3. Join 2¼"-wide black-and-gold bubble print strips into 1 continuous piece for straight-grain French-fold binding. Add binding to quilt.

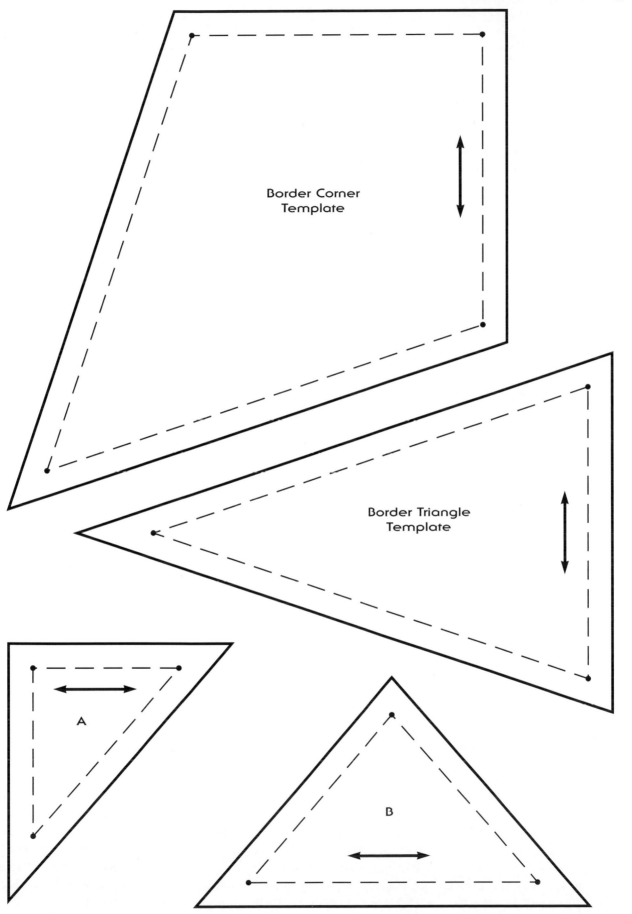

Border Corner
Template

Border Triangle
Template

A

B

Patches

Quilter Marty Freed combined appliquéd crazy hearts with basic Nine-Patch blocks to make this attractive quilt.

Finished Size: 73½" x 90¼"
Blocks: 48 (6") Nine-Patch
Blocks
35 (6") Heart Blocks

Materials
4¼ yards beige print for
    background
30 fat eighths* dark prints
8 fat eighths* light prints
6 yards fabric for backing
¾ yard fabric for binding
Freezer paper
Queen-size batting
*Fat eighth = 9" x 22"

Cutting
Measurements include ¼"
seam allowances. Cut crosswise strips unless otherwise
noted. Patterns are on page
119.

From beige print, cut:
• 1 (69"-long) piece. Cut this
  into:
    • 4 (9" x 68¼") lengthwise
    borders.
    • 8 (2⅜") squares. Cut
    squares in half diagonally to
    make 16 corner triangles for
    pieced borders.
• 6 (6½"-wide) strips. Cut strips
into 35 (6½") squares for
heart backgrounds.
• 6 (4⅛"-wide) strips. Cut
strips into 54 (4⅛") squares.
Cut squares in quarters
diagonally to make 216 side
triangles for borders.
• 2 (9¾"-wide) strips. Cut strips
into 6 (9¾") squares and 2
(5⅛") squares. Cut 9¾"
squares in quarters diagonally to make 24 side triangles
for quilt center. Cut 5⅛"
squares in half diagonally to
make 4 corner triangles for
quilt center.

From dark fat eighths, cut:
• 12 (2½") squares from *each*
  fat eighth, for a total of 360
  squares. (You will have 8
  extra.)
• 4 large hearts (A).
• 24 small hearts (B).
• 4 leaves (C) and 4 leaves (C
  rev.).
• 4 buds (D).
• Reserve scraps for making
  heart blocks.

From each light fat eighth, cut:
• 24 (2½") squares for a total
  of 192 squares.

From freezer paper, cut:
• 35 (5") squares. Then cut 1
  large heart (A) from each
  square.

From binding fabric, cut:
• 11 (2¼"-wide) strips.

Heart Block Assembly
1. Foundation-piece dark print
scraps onto paper heart foundation, making sure scraps
extend at least ¼" beyond
paper edge. Trim around
heart, leaving seam allowance
to turn under for appliqué.
2. Repeat to make 35 hearts.
3. Fold 1 (6½") beige print
square in quarters diagonally
and finger-press to find center.
Unfold. Center 1 heart on
square and appliqué by hand
or machine. Repeat for
remaining hearts.
4. Carefully trim fabric behind
hearts and remove freezer
paper.

Nine-Patch Block Assembly
1. Select 9 (2½") squares as
follows: 4 of a light print, 4 of
a dark print, and 1 of a ➤

different dark print.

2. Referring to photo and to *Quilt Top Assembly Diagram* for color placement, join squares in 3 rows of 3 squares each. Join rows.

3. Repeat to make 48 Nine-Patch blocks.

Quilt Assembly

1. Referring to *Quilt Top Assembly Diagram*, join Heart blocks, Nine-Patch blocks, side triangles, and corner triangles in diagonal rows as shown.

2. Join rows.

3. Fold 1 beige print border in half vertically and horizontally; fingerpress to find center. Unfold.

4. Referring to photo for placement, appliqué 5 small hearts (B) to center of each border.

5. Center and sew 1 border strip to each side of quilt. Repeat for top and bottom of quilt.

6. Referring to photo for placement, position and appliqué 1 bud (D), 1 large heart (A), 1 leaf (C), 1 leaf (C rev.) and 1 small heart (B) at corner as shown. Repeat for all corners.

Pieced Border Assembly

1. To make 1 side border, join 30 (2½") dark squares, 58 beige print side triangles for border, and 4 beige print corner triangles for border as shown in *Border Assembly Diagram.*

2. Repeat to make second side border.

3. To make top border, join 26 (2½") dark squares, 50 beige print side triangles for border, and 4 beige print corner trian-

gles for border as shown in *Border Assembly Diagram.*

4. Repeat to make bottom border.

5. Add borders to top and bottom of quilt.

Quilting and Finishing

1. Cut backing fabric into 2 (3-yard) pieces. Join lengthwise

to form backing. Press seam allowance to 1 side.

2. Layer backing, batting, and quilt top; baste. Quilt as desired. Quilt shown has allover meander quilting.

3. Join 2¼"-wide strips into 1 continuous piece to make straight-grain French-fold binding. Add binding to quilt.

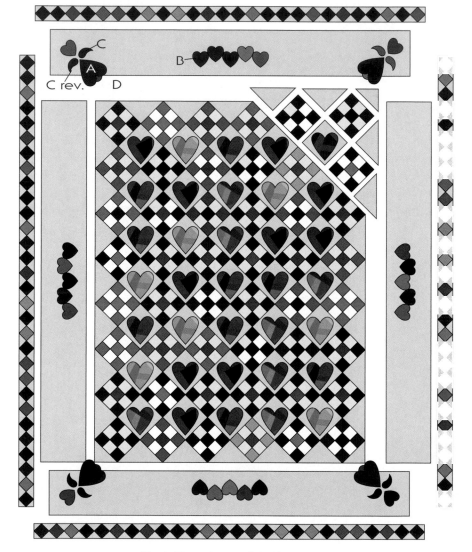

Quilt Top Assembly Diagram

Border Assembly Diagram

Leaf
C

Leaf
C rev.

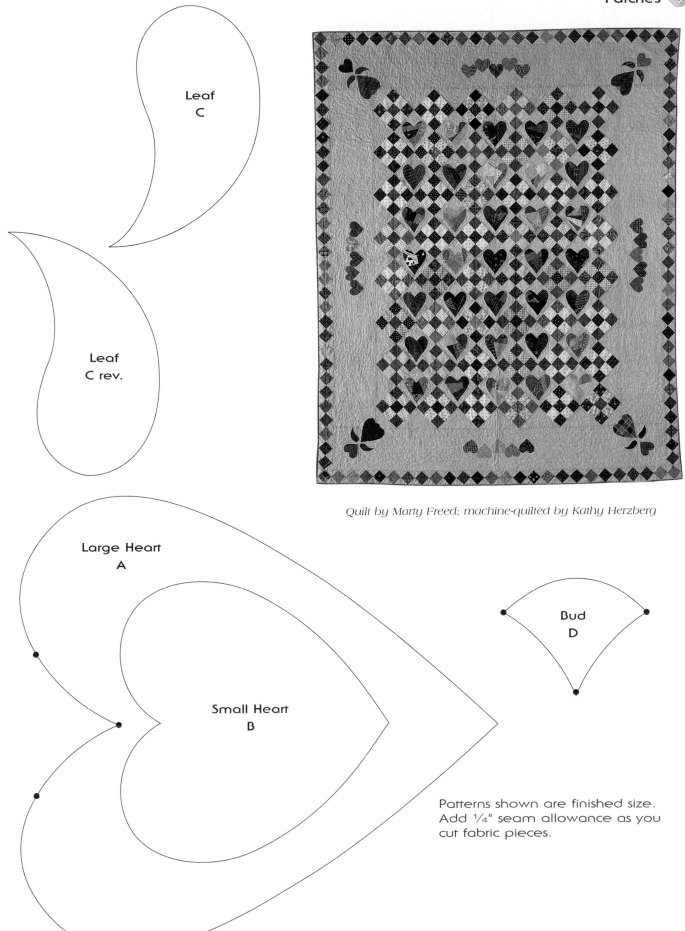

Quilt by Marty Freed; machine-quilted by Kathy Herzberg

Large Heart
A

Small Heart
B

Bud
D

Patterns shown are finished size.
Add ¼" seam allowance as you
cut fabric pieces.

Cumberland Compass

Cindy Erickson fell in love with Fons & Porter's Cumberland Collection by Benartex. "I bought a little of each fabric, knowing they would look perfect in a Mariner's Compass quilt," she says. "I designed the setting on my computer, and then I selected the pieces for each compass randomly. I love the way the values mixed! It made some of the blocks appear to be different patterns."

Finished Size: 85" x 85"
Blocks: 25 (12") Mariner's
Compass Blocks

Materials
25 fat quarters* assorted medium to dark prints from Cumberland Collection or other fabrics
9 yards cream print for background
3 yards large dark print for sashing triangles and binding
1¼ yards light brown print for setting triangles
7½ yards fabric for backing
Queen-size batting
Freezer paper or other template material
12½" square (or larger) rotary-cutting ruler
*Fat quarter = 18" x 22"

Cutting
Measurements include ¼" seam allowances. Use patterns on pages 123–125 to make templates.

From assorted prints, choose 4 at random:
• Fabric #1—Cut 4 As and 1 F.
• Fabric #2—Cut 4 Bs.

• Fabric #3—Cut 8 Cs.
• Fabric #4—Cut 16 Ds.
Repeat to cut 25 sets.

From cream print, cut:
• 9 (13"-wide) strips. Cut strips into 25 (13") squares for compass blocks. (Blocks will be trimmed after appliqué is completed.)
• 800 Es.
• 256 Gs.
• 256 G rev.
• 2 (3⅞"-wide) strips. Cut strips into 20 (3⅞") squares. Cut squares in half diagonally to make 40 half-square triangles (24 for sashing corners and 16 for sashing row ends).

From large dark print, cut:
• 2 (3⅞"-wide) strips. Cut strips into 12 (3⅞") squares. Cut squares in half diagonally to make 24 half-square triangles for sashing corners.
• 256 Hs.
• 9 (2¼"-wide) strips for binding.

From light brown print, cut:
• 2 (18¼"-wide) strips. Cut strips into 3 (18¼") squares. Cut squares in quarters diagonally to make 12 side

setting triangles.
• 2 (9⅜") squares. Cut squares in half diagonally to make 4 corner setting triangles.

Mariner's Compass Block Assembly
1. Choose 32 Es and 1 set of compass pieces A–D and F.
2. Join 1 E to each side of 1 D, as shown in *D/E Unit Assembly Diagram*. Press seams away from D. Make 16 D/E units.
3. Join 1 D/E unit to each side of 1 C, as shown in *C/D/E Unit Assembly Diagram*. Press seams away from C. Make 8 C units. ➡

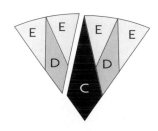

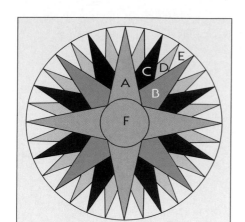

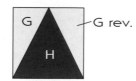

Sashing Square Diagram

Sashing Unit Diagram

Sashing Corner Diagram

4. In a similar manner, join 1 C unit to each side of 1 B. Press seams away from B. Make 4 B units.

5. Join 1 B unit to each side of 1 A. Press seams away from A. Make 2 A units.

6. Join A units to remaining A pieces to form circle, as shown in *Block Diagram*. Press flat.

7. Appliqué F to center.

8. Fold 13" background square into quarters and press to make guidelines. Pin compass in position, aligning A points with creases, and appliqué. Carefully trim background fabric behind compass, leaving ¼" seam allowance.

9. Trim block to 12½" square.

10. Make 25 Mariner's Compass blocks.

Sashing Block Assembly

1. Join 1 G and 1 G rev. to each side of 1 H to make 1 sashing square (*Sashing Square Diagram*). Block should measure 3½" square.

2. Make 256 sashing squares. Join into 4-block sashing units as shown in *Sashing Unit Diagram*.

3. Join 1 dark half-square triangle to 1 cream half-square

triangle to make a square, as shown in *Sashing Corner Diagram*. Make 24 sashing corners.

Quilt Assembly

1. Lay out pieces as shown in *Quilt Top Assembly Diagram*. Remaining cream half-square triangles go at ends of sashing rows.

2. Join into diagonal rows; join rows to complete quilt top.

Quilting and Finishing

1. Divide backing fabric into 3 (2½-yard) lengths. Cut 1 piece in half lengthwise. Sew 1 narrow panel between 2 wide panels. Press seam allowances toward narrow panel. Remaining narrow panel is extra.

2. Layer backing, batting, and quilt top; baste. Quilt as desired. Quilt shown was quilted through compass points in straight lines. Sashing triangles have curved outline quilting, and outer setting triangles are filled with outline quilting.

3. Join 2¼"-wide dark print strips into 1 continuous piece for straight-grain French-fold binding. Add binding to quilt.

Corner Triangle · Sashing Unit · Side Setting Triangle

Quilt Top Assembly Diagram

Using Freezer Paper

Using freezer paper for templates can be helpful when you need precision piecing, as in the Mariner's Compass Block.

A

B

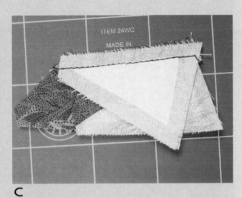

C

1. Trace finished-size patterns (without seam allowance) onto paper side of freezer paper and cut them out (photo A). You will need a separate template for each fabric piece.
2. Use a dry iron to press shiny side of templates to wrong side of fabric, spacing at least ½" apart. Cut out with a rotary cutter and ruler, adding ¼" seam allowance to each piece (photo B).
3. As you join pieces for block assembly, align freezer-

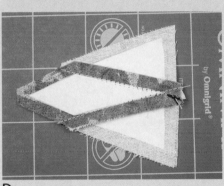

D

E

paper edges and sew along that edge (photo C).
4. Continue adding pieces. Leave freezer paper in place

as a guide while you sew (photos D and E).
5. Remove freezer paper once block is complete.

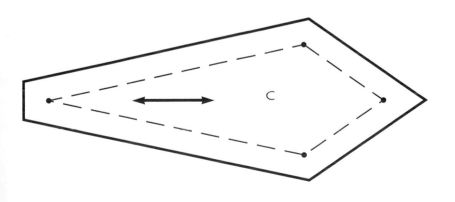

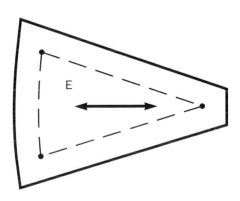

Quilt by Cindy Erickson

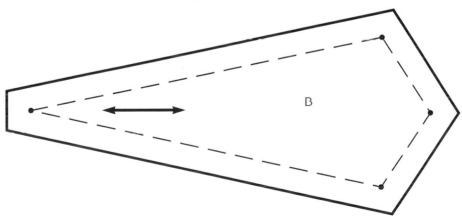

B

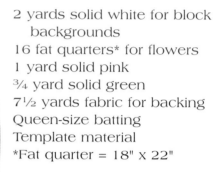

Nosegay

You might recognize this traditional Depression-era block by such names as Bride's Bouquet and Old-fashioned Nosegay. This classic design has been a favorite among quiltmakers for many generations. This quilt is from Liz Porter's collection.

Finished Size: 80" x 97"
Blocks: 20 (12") Nosegay
Blocks

Materials
5½ yards solid yellow for setting pieces, borders, and binding

2 yards solid white for block backgrounds
16 fat quarters* for flowers
1 yard solid pink
¾ yard solid green
7½ yards fabric for backing
Queen-size batting
Template material
*Fat quarter = 18" x 22"

Cutting
Measurements include ¼" seam allowances. Cut crosswise strips unless otherwise noted. Patterns for block pieces are on pages 128–129.

From solid yellow, cut:
- 4 (6½" x 99") strips for borders.
- 12 (12½") setting squares.
- 4 (18¼") squares. Cut each square in quarters diagonally to make 14 setting triangles (you will have 2 extra).
- 2 (9⅜") squares. Cut each square in half diagonally to make 4 corner triangles.
- Cut remaining fabric into 2¼"-wide strips for binding.

*T*o cut reversed pieces for shapes such as F, position template wrong side up when marking fabric. —Liz

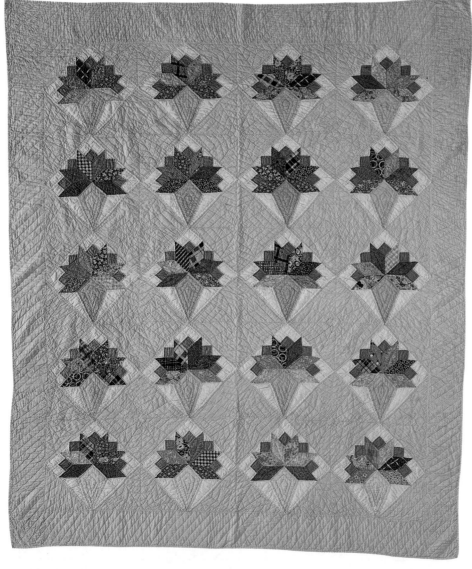

From solid white, cut:
- 4 (2¼"-wide) strips. Cut strips into 60 (2¼") squares (C).
- 6 (2¼"-wide) strips. Cut strips into 60 (2¼" x 4") rectangles (D).
- 2 (3¾"-wide) strips. Cut strips into 20 (3¾") squares. Cut squares in quarters diagonally to make 80 quarter-square triangles (E).
- 20 Fs and 20 F rev.

From assorted prints, cut:
- 120 As.

From solid pink, cut:
- 20 Bs.

From solid green, cut:
- 6 (2¼"-wide) strips. Cut strips into 100 (2¼") squares (C).

Block Assembly
Refer to *Block Diagram* throughout.

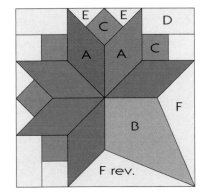

Block Diagram

Trace, scan, or photocopy this quilt label to finish your quilt.

As you assemble the block pieces, pin-match pieces at corner matching dot marks. Accurate piecing is critical so that blocks will lie flat. Stitch only from dot to dot, backstitching at the beginning and end of seams. This leaves the seam allowances free so you can set in other pieces smoothly. —Liz

1. Join 6 As and 1 B to form nosegay.
2. Make 1 pieced square by joining 1 green C, 1 white C, and 1 white D as shown. Make 3 pieced squares.
3. Make 1 pieced triangle by joining 1 green C and 2 white Es as shown. Make 2 pieced triangles.
4. Set pieced squares and triangles into openings between As as shown.
5. Set F and F rev. into openings along sides of B.
6. Make 20 Nosegay blocks.

Quilt Assembly
1. Referring to *Quilt Top Assembly Diagram*, lay out blocks on point in 5 horizontal rows with 4 blocks in each row. Fill in spaces between blocks with setting squares as shown. Fill in openings around outside edges with setting triangles and corner triangles.
2. Join blocks and setting pieces in diagonal rows. Press seam allowances toward setting pieces. Join rows.
3. Measure quilt length and trim 2 borders to this measurement. Join borders to sides of quilt top. Measure quilt width, including side borders, and trim remaining 2 borders to this measurement. Join borders to top and bottom edges. Press seam allowances toward borders.

Quilting and Finishing
1. Divide backing fabric into 3 (2½-yard) panels. Join panels to make quilt back. Seams will run parallel to top and bottom edges of quilt.
2. Layer backing, batting, and quilt top. Baste.
3. Quilt as desired. Suggested quilting for B is indicated on pattern piece.
4. Join 2¼"-wide yellow strips into 1 continuous piece to make straight-grain French-fold binding. Add binding to quilt.

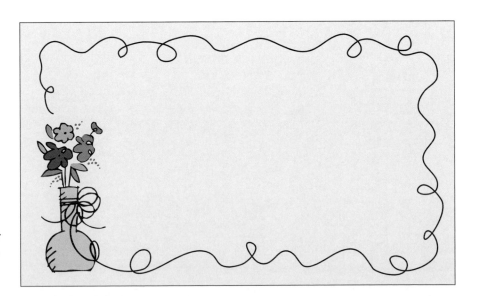

Quilt Top Assembly Diagram

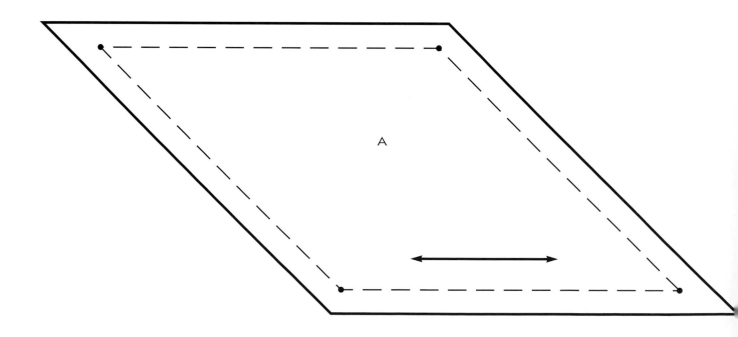

A

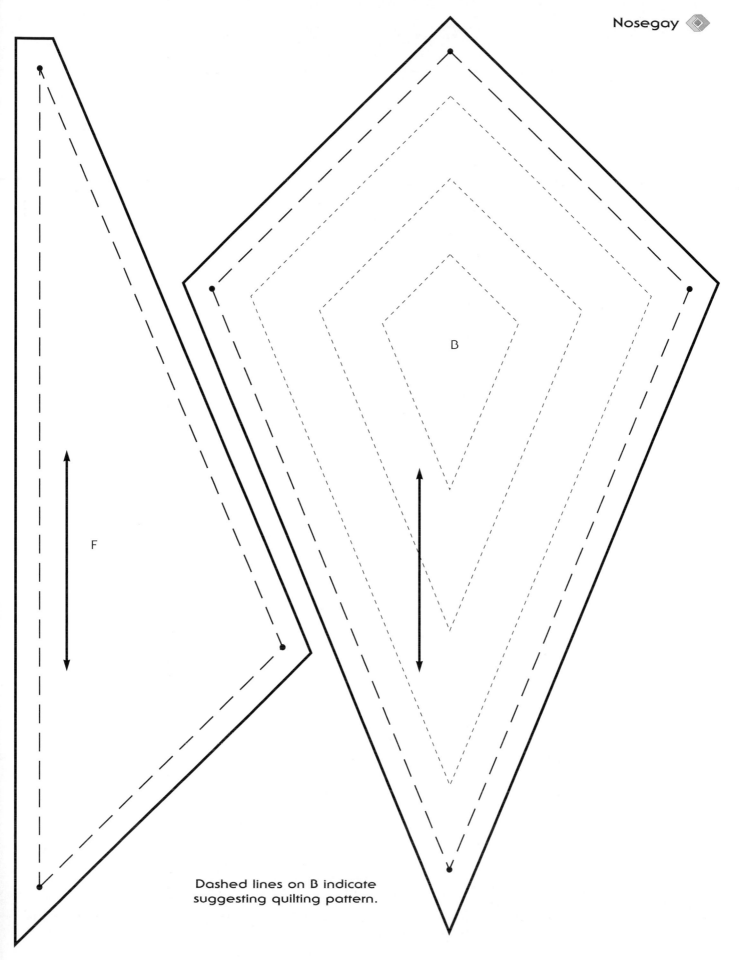

F

B

Dashed lines on B indicate
suggesting quilting pattern.

◈ In the Sewing Room ◈

TAKING STOCK

Having the right tools will increase your enjoyment of quilting and improve your accuracy. New products are constantly appearing on the market, but below is a list of must-haves to get you started.

Cutting Tools

Rotary Cutter: Purchase a cutter with at least a 2"-diameter blade. The larger cutters allow you to cut through more layers. Look at the instructions on the back of the package to see the proper way to hold the brand you bought.

Cutting Mat: Purchase the largest mat you can afford. Make sure you at least have one that measures 18" x 24".

Cutting Rulers: The longer you quilt, the more of these you will buy. Start with a 6" x 24" ruler. Later you may want to add a 6" square, a 12½" square, and a triangle ruler.

Cutting Table: Make your worktable a comfortable height for standing while you cut and work. Most people like a cutting table about 36" high. Some tables are available with collapsible sides to conserve space when not in use.

Thread Clippers: Trim threads quickly with this spring-action tool.

Fabric Shears: A fine pair of sharp fabric shears will become one of your treasured possessions. To keep them sharp, do not cut anything but fabric with them.

Paper Scissors: Use an inexpensive pair of large, sharp scissors to cut paper, template plastic, and cardboard—everything except fabric.

Appliqué Scissors: The duckbill piece at the bottom helps you to trim background fabrics away from appliqué shapes.

Walking foot

Walking Foot: If you plan to machine-quilt, you must have a walking foot to feed the quilt layers through your machine evenly.

Thread: Use cotton thread for piecing and quilting. You'll find that neutral colors—white, beige, or gray—works with most quilts.

Pins: Spend a few extra dollars to get fine silk pins. These pins are so thin, you can usually keep them in your fabric and sew over them with most sewing machines.

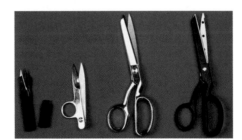
Shown from left to right: thread clippers, fabric shears, paper scissors, and appliqué scissors

Sewing Tools

Sewing Machine: Unless you plan to do machine appliqué, a good straight-stitch sewing machine is all you'll need.

Needles: Replace the needle in your sewing machine regularly. Size 80/12 is just right for machine piecing. For handwork, use a size 10 or 11 sharp for hand appliqué and a 10 or 12 between for hand quilting.

Portable steam iron

Pressing Tools

Iron: Look for a steam iron that produces plenty of steam.

Plastic Squirt Bottle: Some fabrics need a spray of water in addition to the steam from the iron.

Ironing Board: An ironing board or large pressing pad at one end of your cutting table will enable you to stand and to press at a comfortable height.

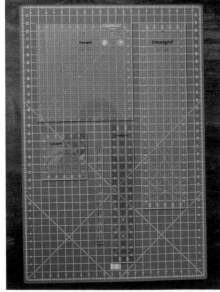
Large mat and various rulers

Organizing a Signature Quilt & Making Templates

ORGANIZING A SIGNATURE QUILT

If you will be making all the blocks yourself, stabilize the signature pieces (see page 133) and distribute them to your friends. It a group of quilters will be making the blocks, make sure you give them instructions for the block you choose.

- If the quilt will have a uniform background (as opposed to scrappy), buy more of that fabric than you need. That way, you can cut more pieces if some get lost or soiled.
- Purchase several Pigma™ pens. We recommend using the .05 width. The tip is wider than the .01 size, making the writing more visible and less likely to fade in the wash.
- Decide how many blocks you need and make a list of all participants.
- Mark people off your list as they return their signature piece or quilt block so that you'll know who to follow up with.
- If quilters are making blocks for you, be sure to set a theme for the quilt, whether by color or fabric type. If you simply ask them to use their favorite fabrics, you'll end up with neons, reproduction prints, and novelty prints, and the quilt will lack cohesiveness.
- If the quilt will be a gift, try to use colors to suit that person's taste, not yours.

ADAPTING THE QUILT SIZE

If the quilt you plan to make is not the size you want, there are several ways to adapt the design.

To make a smaller quilt, eliminate a row of blocks, set the blocks without sashing, and/or narrow the border widths.

To make a larger quilt, add rows of blocks, sashing, and/or multiple borders. Each addition requires extra yardage, which you should estimate before you buy fabric.

HOW TO USE OUR PATTERNS

Oxmoor House patterns are full size. Patterns for pieced blocks show the seam line (dashed) and the cutting line (solid). Appliqué patterns do not include seam allowances.

MAKING TEMPLATES

Almost all of the quilts in this book can be made with rotary-cutting instructions. However, a few do require templates. You can make templates from traditional template plastic or from cardboard.

However, we have found a new product that allows you to make your own templates and still use a rotary cutter to cut

Cut-Your Own Templates Kit

the fabric! Designed by John Flynn, Cut-Your-Own Templates™ are made of formica (see Resources on page 144). The kit includes several sheets of formica and everything you need to make any template shape. The formica is thick enough that you can use your rotary cutter to cut along its edge. This set is ideal for making quilts like *Nosegay* on page 126.

APPLIQUÉ

Appliqué is the process of sewing pieces onto a background to create a fabric picture.

Hand Appliqué

For traditional hand appliqué, use the drawn line as

Use the drawn line as a guide.

Slipstitch around each piece.

a guide to turn under seam allowances on each piece. Do not turn an edge that will be covered by another piece. Hand-baste the seam allowances. You can eliminate basting, if you prefer, and rely on rolling the edge under with the tip of your needle as you sew. This is called needle-turned appliqué. Pin appliqué

Appliqué

pieces to the background.

Slipstitch around each piece, using thread that matches the appliqué. (We used contrasting thread for photography.) Pull the needle through the background and catch a few threads on the fold of the appliqué. Reinsert the needle into the background and bring the needle up through the appliqué for the next stitch. Make close, tiny stitches that do not show on the right side. Remove basting.

Freezer-Paper Appliqué

In using this technique, the finished appliqué will be a mirror image of the pattern. So, if the pattern is an irregular shape (not symmetrical), first reverse the pattern. Trace a full-size pattern onto the paper (nonwaxy) side of freezer paper. Cut out each freezer-paper template along the drawn lines.

When you press the seam allowances over the freezer paper, we recommend using a product called GluTube®. If you've ever used a glue stick with freezer paper to temporarily "baste" the seam allowances, you'll discover that GluTube® works much the same way. However, it is not gooey once it dries, and it will not stick to your fingers and make a mess like a glue stick can. It also allows you to create sharp, smooth edges on your appliqué. Here's how it works:

1. Press the freezer-paper template to the wrong side of the appliqué fabric.
2. Apply GluTube® in a circular motion, covering approximately ¼" of the edges along both the template and the fabric. Let the

Step 1

Step 2

Step 3

Step 4

Step 5

glue dry for a few minutes.

3. Cut out the template, adding ¼" seam allowance. Don't worry about cutting into the glue—once dry, it has the same consistency as the adhesive on yellow sticky notes.
4. Clip curves or points as needed. Using a straight pin, fold the seam allowances over the edge of the template. Use your fingers to gently set the temporary bond. You may lift and reposition the fabric as needed.
5. Appliqué the shape to the background as usual. Clip the background fabric from behind the appliquéd shape and gently remove the freezer paper with tweezers. The template will release easily.

GluTube® is available in quilt shops and mail-order catalogs (see Resources, page 144).

Fusible Appliqué

If you do not enjoy handwork, fusing appliqué shapes with paper-backed fusible web may be an option for you. Follow manufacturer's instructions on the package. You will still need to cover the fabric edges so that they will not ravel when the quilt is washed. You can do this with a machine satin stitch or with a hand or machine blanket-stitch.

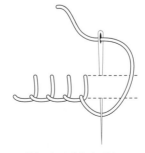
Blanket Stitch Diagram

Signing Blocks & Using Rubber Stamps

SIGNING BLOCKS

To sign blocks, you will need freezer paper (available in grocery stores near the aluminum foil) and colorfast, fabric-safe pens (see Resources on page 144).

1. To stabilize the fabric for writing, press a piece of freezer paper to the back.

2. Use a thick-pointed permanent pen to draw a line on the paper side of the freezer paper to give you a writing guideline that will be visible through the fabric.

3. Using a colorfast, fabric-safe pen (like Pigma™), write lightly and slowly to allow the ink to flow and to prevent the pen from catching in the weave of the cloth (fabric is rougher than paper). Let the ink dry.

4. Heat-set the ink with a hot, dry iron on the back of the fabric.

Use rubber stamps for creative labels.

USING RUBBER STAMPS

Stamping is a fun and easy way to add decoration and documentation to your quilts. In adapting stamping to our quilts, we are joining a historic tradition of quilt decoration. Quilters of the mid-nineteenth century used stamps to embellish their signature quilts.

To successfully stamp on fabric, the stamp design must be deeply etched into the rubber. Many stamps designed for paper stamping are not deeply etched. As a result, the image may be pale and the details lost on fabric. Stamps made by Susan McKelvey (see Resources, page 144) meet these requirements, and several of her stamps were used on quilts in this book.

Make sure that the ink you use is colorfast and fabric-safe. We recommend Fabrico™ ink, which is available in 12 colors on preinked stamp pads (see Resources, page 144).

STAMPING BLOCKS

Practice on a fabric scrap to see how much ink you need and how much pressure to apply. Stamp on a hard, flat surface.

1. When inking the stamp, hold the stamp up and the stamp pad down as shown in Photo A. This enables you to control how much ink you put on the stamp.

Photo A: Hold the stamp under the pad while inking.

2. Tap the pad gently against the stamp. Press lightly several times, rather than hard once, to prevent applying excess ink.

3. Stamp the fabric by pressing firmly; don't rock the stamp.

4. Let the ink dry. It dries quickly to the touch (Photo B).

Photo B: The finished results look professional.

5. Heat-set the ink with a hot, dry iron on the back of the fabric.

Using Computers

USING COMPUTERS

If you own a home computer, try using it to print designs on your blocks and quilt labels. If you don't like your handwriting, or if you just want to add some creative lettering, your computer will have a wide range of fonts to choose from. Below is a quick review of terms to help get you started. Most of these items will be under the "Style" menu at the top of your computer screen. Because brands differ, these are only general descriptions to get you started. You will need to use your computer manual or consult your computer dealer if you need specific information.

Useful Things to Know

A font is the print style you use for the letters. Most word processing programs will come with a wide variety of fonts. Regardless of the font you choose, you can make it bold or italic, if desired.

The size determines how large your fonts will be. Normally, you don't want to use a size smaller than 10 or 12 points (pt) for the text to be read easily. Experiment to see how large you can go. For a quilt label, you might consider putting the quilt's name in 36 pt; your name, date, and residence in 24 pt; and the text describing the quilt in 12 pt. (See the label above.)

Depending on whether or not you have a color printer, you can print items in color. However, run a test to see if your printer has colorfast ink. Most do not, although most black inks tend to be colorfast. Check with your computer dealer to see if colorfast ink is available for your printer.

Never use noncolorfast ink in a quilt block. However, if you choose to use it for a quilt label, be sure to print yourself a small note in red at the bottom of the label reminding you to remove it before laundering. A better option is to print the design in colorfast black and then color in with Pigma™ pens.

Most computers also come with clipart. If not, the software is widely available (and inexpensive) at office supply and computer stores.

You may also obtain images and fonts from the Internet. Download the images onto your computer. Watch for charges, though. There are many items you can download free, so only pay for fonts you really love.

Don't be afraid of the Internet. Unless you are asked to enter a credit card number, you will not be charged for the fonts. Some sites allow you to download fonts free for 30 days. At the end of that time, they simply disappear from your computer.

If you own a scanner, your possibilities are nearly endless. Any image you can scan can be transferred to fabric.

Printing on Fabric

You can print what's on your screen directly onto your fabric. You are not limited to muslin; you can use any 100% cotton fabric, as long as it is light enough for the ink to show. *Note: Oxmoor House does not assume any responsibility for damage caused to your printer trying these techniques. If your printer jams on paper, do not try to feed it fabric. Do not use these techniques at work with equipment that is not your own.*

The quilt labels shown in this book were made on a Windows 95 compatible home PC, using an HP Inkjet 820 color printer. The text came from Microsoft Works™ for Windows 95, and the clipart is Microsoft ClipArt Gallery 2.0.
1. Design a quilt label on your screen. Enter text in your favorite font, varying the size as desired.
2. Under your menu bar, find "Insert" and scroll down to "Clipart." Select the desired image, and click on "OK" or "Insert" (Photo A). The image should now be in your quilt

Using Computers

Photo A

Photo C

Photo F

Photo B

Photo D

Photo G

Photo E

New products make printing computer images to fabric fast and easy.

label text (Photo B).

3. Adjust text and image sizes as needed. Print a sample on paper to see if you're happy with it. Experiment to determine if your paper feeds into the printer faceup or facedown.

4. Using an old rotary cutter, cut a piece of freezer paper 8½" x 11" (Photo C). Using a hot, dry iron, press freezer paper to the wrong side of the fabric (Photo D).

5. Using your good rotary cutter, trim the fabric to 8½" x 11" (Photo E). Press outside edges again, to make sure the freezer paper is still secure. Check for extraneous threads along the edges and clip them, if needed.

6. Place the fabric sheet on top of the paper in your printer (Photo F).

7. Click on "Print." Your fabric should feed through the printer as paper would (Photo G).

8. Let the ink dry. Remove the freezer paper and then heat-set

the ink with a hot, dry iron. Trim the image to size, if necessary.

There is a new product available called Computer Printer Fabric™ that feeds directly into your printer. Check local quilting and computer shops or order it from Connecting Threads (see Resources, page 144). It is available in white and cream.

June Tailor also has a new printer fabric that is colorfast and washable. Regardless of whether your printer has colorfast ink or not, any image printed is permanent after eight hours. See page 144.

Joining Blocks and Borders

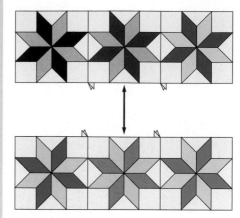

Straight Set

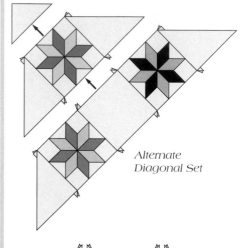

Alternate Diagonal Set

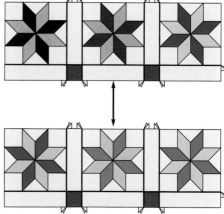

Sashed Blocks

JOINING BLOCKS

Arrange blocks and setting pieces on the floor, on a large table, or on a design wall. Identify the pieces in each row and verify the position of each block. This is the fun part—move the blocks around to find the best balance of color and value. Don't begin sewing until you're happy with the placement of each block.

1. Press seam allowances between blocks in a straight set in the same direction. From row to row, press in opposite directions so that seam allowances will offset when you join rows.

2. In an alternate set, straight or diagonal, press seam allowances between blocks toward setting squares or triangles. This creates the least bulk and always results in opposing seam allowances when you join adjacent rows.

3. Sashing eliminates questions about pressing. Just remember to always press toward the sashing. Assemble rows with sashing strips between blocks, pressing each new seam allowance toward the sashing. If necessary, ease the block to match the strip. Assemble the quilt with sashing rows between block rows.

BORDERS

Most quilts have borders, which help frame the quilt. They can be plain, pieced, or appliquéd, with square or mitered corners.

Measuring

It's common for one side of a quilt top to be slightly different from the measurement on the opposite side. Even small discrepancies in cutting and piecing add up across the quilt. Sewing borders of equal length to opposite sides will square up the quilt.

When you cut lengthwise strips for borders, you'll want

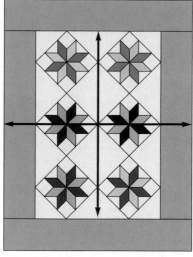

Measuring for Square Corners

to measure your quilt before trimming the strips to the size indicated in the instructions. When you measure, measure down the center of the quilt rather than along the edges.

Square Corners

Measure from top to bottom through the middle of the quilt as shown above. Trim side borders to this length and add them to the quilt sides. You may need to ease one side of a quilt to fit the border and stretch the opposite side to fit the same border length. In the end, both sides will be the same. Unless you're using a walking foot, your sewing machine naturally feeds the bottom layer through the feed dogs faster than it does the top layer. So always put the longer side (the side that needs to be eased in) on the bottom as you sew.

For top and bottom borders, measure from side to side through the middle of the quilt, including the side borders you just added and their seam allowance. Trim remaining border to this measurement and add them to the quilt.

Mitered Corners

Measuring for Mitered Borders

Press the mitered corner seam flat.

Mitered Corners

The seam of a mitered corner is more subtle than that of a square corner, so it creates the illusion of a continuous line around the quilt. Mitered corners are ideal for striped borders, pieced borders, or multiple plain borders. Sew multiple borders together first and treat the resulting striped unit as a single border for mitering.

Sewing a Mitered Corner

1. Measure your quilt as described above. Add to this measurement the width of the border plus 2".
2. Place a pin on the center of the quilt side and another pin on the center of the border.
3. With right sides facing and raw edges aligned, match the pins on the border to the quilt. Working from the center out, pin border to quilt. The border will extend beyond the quilt edges. Do not trim it.
4. Sew border to quilt, backstitching at each end. Press seam allowance toward border. Join remaining borders in the same manner.

5. With right sides facing, fold the quilt diagonally as shown in Mitering Diagram 1, aligning the raw edges of adjacent borders. Pin securely.
6. Align a ruler along the diagonal fold as shown in Mitering Diagram 2. Holding the ruler firmly, mark a line from the end of the border seam to the raw edge.
7. Start machine-stitching at the beginning of the marked line, backstitch, and then stitch on the line out to the raw edge.
8. Unfold the quilt to be sure that the corner lies flat. Correct the stitching if necessary. Trim the seam allowance to ¼".
9. Miter the remaining corners. Press the corner seams flat.

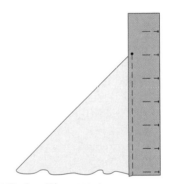

Mitering Diagram 1

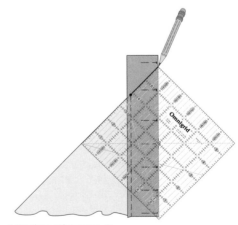

Mitering Diagram 2

Preparing for Quilting

PREPARING FOR QUILTING

The quilting design is an important part of any quilt, so choose it with care. The hours you spend stitching together the layers of your quilt create shadows and depths that bring the quilt to life, so make the design count.

In our "Quilting and Finishing" instructions, we tell you to "quilt as desired," but then we also tell you how the project shown was quilted. Since most of the intricate quilting designs were used from purchased stencils, we cannot reproduce the pattern within the book.

Quilting Without Marking

There are several ways to quilt that do not require you to mark the quilt top:

- In-the-ditch: Quilting right in the seam.
- Outline Quilting: Quilting 1/4" from the seam line. You can "eyeball" this measurement or use 1/4"-wide masking tape as a guide.
- Grid Quilting: Quilting in straight, diagonal lines, usually 1" apart. Using the 45° line on your ruler to get you started, place 1"-wide masking tape on your quilt and quilt along its edge. Never keep the tape on your quilt for long periods of time—if you must set your project aside for a time, remove the tape.
- Stippling: Freestyle, meandering lines of quilting worked closely together to fill open areas.

Using Stencils

To find a stencil for a quilting design, check your local quilt

Using a stencil to mark a quilt design

shop or mail-order catalogs (see Resources, page 144) for one that suits your quilt.

To transfer a design to the quilt top, position the stencil on the quilt and mark through the slits in the stencil. Connect the lines after removing the stencil.

Before using any marker, test it on scraps to be sure marks will wash out. Don't use just any pencil. There are many

pencils and chalk markers available that are designed to wash out.

BATTING

Precut batting comes in five sizes. The precut batting listed for each quilt is the most suitable for the quilt's finished size. Some stores sell 90" batting by the yard, which might be more practical for your quilt.

Loft is the height or thickness of the batting. For a traditional, flat look, choose low-loft cotton batting. Thick batting is difficult to quilt, unless you plan to machine-quilt or tie it as a comforter.

Cotton batting provides the flat, thin look of an antique quilt, making it ideal for memo-

Layering a quilt

ry quilts. Cotton shrinks slightly when washed, giving it that wrinkled look characteristic of all quilts.

Polyester batting is easy to stitch and can be washed with little shrinkage. However, look for the word "bonded" when selecting polyester batts. Bonding keeps the loft of the batt uniform and reduces the effects of bearding (migration of loose fibers through the quilt top). Avoid bonded batts that feel stiff.

BACKING

The instructions in this book tell you how to cut and piece standard 42"-wide fabric to make backing. The backing should be at lcast 3" larger than the top on all sides.

For a large quilt, 90"- or 108"-wide fabric is a scnsible option that reduces waste and eliminates backing seams. Quilters are no longer limited to muslin; new wide fabrics are available in lovely prints.

Some quilters treat the backing as another design element of their quilt, choosing to piece interesting designs or appliqué large shapes.

LAYERING

Lay the backing right side down on a large work surface—a large table, two tables pushed together, or a clean floor. Use masking tape to secure the edges, keeping the backing wrinkle-free and slightly taut.

Smooth the batting over the backing; then trim the batting even with the backing. Center the pressed quilt top right side up on the batting. Make sure the

Thread basting

edges of the backing and quilt top are parallel.

BASTING

Basting keeps layers from shifting during quilting. Baste with a long needle and white thread (colored thread can leave a residue on light fabrics). Or use safety pins, if you prefer.

Start in the center and baste a line of stitches to each corner, making a large X. Then baste parallel lines 6" to 8" apart. Finish with a line of basting $1/4$" from the edge.

Some quilters use nickel-plated safety pins for basting. Pin every 2" to 3". Don't close the pins as you go, as this can pucker the backing. When all pins are in place, remove the tape at the quilt edges. Gently tug the backing as you close each pin so that pleats don't form underneath.

Pin basting

Basting gun

Another popular method is to use a basting gun, which shoots plastic tabs through quilt layers. Use paper-cutting scissors to trim the tabs away after quilting is done.

Hand & Machine Quilting

QUILTING

Quilting is the process of stitching the layers of a quilt together, by hand or by machine. The choice of hand or machine quilting depends on the design of the quilt, how much time you have, and the quilt's intended use. The techniques differ, but the results of both are functional and attractive.

Hand Quilting

To make a stitch, first insert the needle straight down (Photo A). With your other hand under the quilt, feel for the needle point as it pierces the backing. With practice, you'll be able to find the point without pricking your finger.

Roll the needle to a nearly horizontal position (Photo B). Use the thumb of your sewing hand and the underneath hand to pinch a little hill in the fabric as you push the needle back through the quilt top. Gently tug the thread to pop the knot into the quilt. Then rock the needle back to an upright position for the next stitch. Load 3 to 4 stitches on the needle before pulling it through.

With 6" of thread left, tie a knot close to the quilt top. Backstitch; then pop the knot into the batting. Run the thread through the batting and out the top to clip it.

Machine Quilting

If you plan to machine quilt, you must have a walking foot for your sewing machine (Photo C). This allows all the quilt layers to feed through your machine evenly. Use this foot for straight-line quilting.

For free-motion quilting or stippling, you will need a darning foot (Photo D). Lower the feed dogs or cover them. You control the stitch length by manually moving the fabric.

Another option is to have someone who owns a professional quilting machine to quilt your project. Check your quilt shop or guild for local sources.

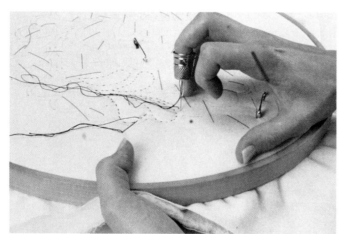
Photo A

Photo C

Photo B

Photo D

Binding

BINDING

There is a common misconception among quilters that quilts must have bias binding. This is not true. The only time a quilt must have bias binding is when it has curved edges or rounded corners. If you use a plaid for the binding and want the plaid to appear "on point," use bias binding.

Most of the quilts in this book have straight edges, so straight-grain French-fold (or double-folded) binding is appropriate for them. This method uses less fabric and can even help your quilt hang straighter.

Making Straight-Grain Binding

1. Cut needed number of strips selvage to selvage. Cut strips 2¼" wide when working with thin batting and 2½" wide when working with thicker fabric (like flannel) or batting.
2. Join strips end-to-end to make a continuous strip. To join 2 strips, layer them perpendicular to each other with right sides facing. Stitch a diagonal seam across strips as shown in Diagram A. Trim seam allowances to ¼" and press open.
3. Fold binding in half lengthwise with wrong sides facing. Press.

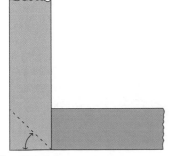

Diagram A

Adding Binding

Sew binding to the front of the quilt first by machine. Begin stitching in the middle of any quilt side. Do not trim excess batting and backing until after you stitch the binding on the quilt.

1. Matching raw edges, lay binding on quilt. Stitch binding to quilt, using ⅜" seam and leaving about 2" unstitched at the top (Diagram B).

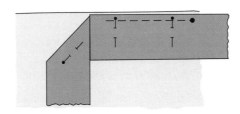

Diagram B

2. Continue stitching down side of quilt. Stop ⅜" from corner and backstitch. Remove quilt from machine and clip threads.
3. Fold binding strip straight up, away from quilt, making a 45° angle (Diagram C).

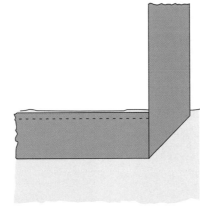

Diagram C

4. Fold binding straight down along next side to be stitched, creating fold that is even with raw edge of previously stitched side.
5. Begin stitching at top edge of new side (Diagram D). Stitch length of new side. Continue

until all 4 corners and sides are joined in this manner. Stop stitching ¼" from point where binding began. Trim excess binding, leaving a 2" tail. Join the 2 tails with diagonal seams (Diagram E). Trim excess binding beyond diagonal stitching and press open. Stitch a straight line (as normal) over this area to secure the ¼" open space (Diagram F).

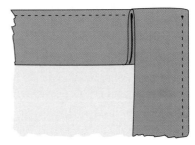

Diagram D

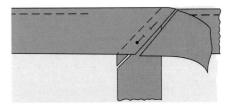

Diagram E

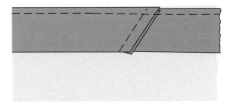

Diagram F

6. Trim excess batting and backing even with binding raw edge.
7. Turn binding over raw edge of quilt and slipstitch in place on backing with matching thread. At each corner, fold binding to form a miter. Whipstitch miter closed. (The miter should form naturally when you turn the corners to the back of the quilt.)

Bias Binding

Making Bias Binding

Step 1

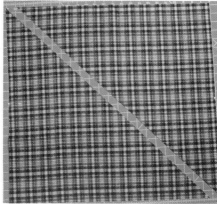

Step 2

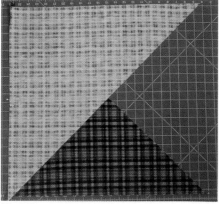

Step 3

1. To cut bias binding, start with a square. (For a queen-size quilt, a 32" square is sufficient.) Center pins at top and bottom edges with heads toward inside. At each side, center a pin with head toward outside edge.

2. Cut square in half diagonally to make 2 triangles.

3. With right sides facing, match edges with pin heads pointed to outside. Remove pins and join triangles with a ¼" seam. Press seam open.

Step 4

Step 5

Step 6

4. On wrong side of fabric, mark cutting lines parallel to long edges. Space between lines would equal the width of the desired strip (for example, 2¼").

5. Match edges with pin heads pointed to inside, right sides facing, offsetting 1 width of binding strip as shown. Join edges with a ¼" seam to make a tube. Press seam open.

6. Begin cutting at extended edge. Follow drawn lines, rolling tube around as you cut, until all fabric is cut into a continuous strip. See instructions on page 141 for adding binding to quilt.

QUILT LABELS

It is unfortunate to come across a quilt in an antique shop with no record of the quilt's history. Every quilt you make should include a quilt label. You can appliqué or piece the label to the back, or include the information in a quilt block on the front.

At a minimum, your quilt label should include:
- the name of the quilt
- your name
- your city and state
- the date of completion, or the date of presentation.

Additional information can include the story behind the quilt, the maker, and/or the recipient. Consider recording how old you were when you made the quilt.

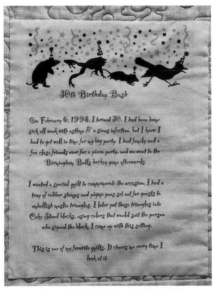

This quilt label explains how the quilt evolved from a 30th birthday party. The signature blocks on the quilt front tell much of the story, but the maker wanted to tell about her birthday party and why she chose the pattern she used for the blocks. She used computer clip art to make the festive image across the top and entered text in the "Party" font below. When she was satisfied with the image on screen, she printed it onto computer printer fabric.

Add Multiple Quilt Labels

Some quilts feature multiple quilt labels. In this example, the quiltmaker started out with a detailed label explaining all the images featured on the front and the stories behind them. Then, as the quilt was exhibited, won awards, and was published, she added more quilt labels. Each label represents an important part of the quilt's history. Future owners will appreciate knowing how the quilt's fame progressed. Just for fun, the maker also appliquéd a chicken to the back.

There are numerous ways to embellish your quilt label. Look for ideas within this book, or use your computer (see page 134) to find images. Rubber stamps can be fun to use, too (see page 133).

You can add more labels if the quilt is displayed, published, or acknowledged with an award.

Even if you purchase an antique quilt, make a label. Research the pattern to see if you can determine the approximate date the quilt was made, or simply put "unknown." But at least put your name and the date and the place you purchased it for future reference.

Resources

Contact the following companies for free catalogs or product information.

COMPUTER SUPPLIES

CompUSA Inc.
Over 200 computer stores
nationwide

CompUSA Net.com Inc.
Online computer superstore for
Internet sales
www.compusanet.com

GENERAL QUILT SUPPLIES AND FABRIC

Fons & Porter Quilt Supply
www.fonsandporter.com

Connecting Threads
P.O. Box 8940
Vancouver, WA 9866-8940
1-800-574-6454

Hancock's of Paducah
3841 Hinkleville Road
Paducah, KY 42001
1-800-845-8723
fax (502) 443-2164
www.Hancocks-Paducah.com

Keepsake Quilting™
P.O. Box 1618
Centre Harbor, NH 03226
1-800-865-9458
www.keepsakequilting.com

Oxmoor House
1-800-633-4910
www.oxmoorhouse.com

Photo Transfer
Colorfast Printer Fabric™
www.junetailor.com
1-800-844-5400

Rotary-Cutting Mats and Rulers
Omnigrid, Inc.
1560 Port Drive
Burlington, WA 98233
1-800-755-3530

Rubber Stamps, Pigma™ Pens, Ink
Wallflower Designs
Susan McKelvey
P.O. Box 307
Royal Oak, MD 21662
Send $3.00 for catalog.

TEMPLATE MATERIAL

Cut-Your-Own Templates
Flynn Quilt Frame Company
1000 Shiloh Overpass Road
Billings, MT 59106
1-800-745-3596
www.flynnquilt.com